A Comparative Quantitative Phonology
of Russian, Czech, and German

by

Henry Kučera

Department of Slavic Languages, Brown University
Providence, Rhode Island

and

George K. Monroe

Department of Languages, Lafayette College
Easton, Pennsylvania

AMERICAN ELSEVIER PUBLISHING COMPANY, Inc.

NEW YORK

1968

SOLE DISTRIBUTORS FOR GREAT BRITAIN
ELSEVIER PUBLISHING COMPANY LTD.
Rippleside Commercial Estate
Barking, Essex, England

SOLE DISTRIBUTORS FOR THE CONTINENT OF EUROPE
ELSEVIER PUBLISHING COMPANY
335 Jan Van Galenstraat, P.O. Box 211
Amsterdam, The Netherlands

Library of Congress Catalog Card Number: 67–28449

PRINTED IN THE UNITED STATES OF AMERICA

PREFACE

The research which is reported and interpreted in this book was carried out, for the most part, at Brown University and at its Computing Laboratory during the last several years. Henry Kučera was responsible for the selection and development of the methods used in the research and for the analysis of the two Slavic languages. George K. Monroe performed the analysis of the German corpus and assisted in the computer processing of the results and in the writing of the text. Both authors shared also the task of preparing the computer programs needed in the project. Henry Kučera is responsible for the final organization and formulation of the book.

It became apparent in the very early stages of this research that any non-elementary quantitative phonological analysis of several languages would require the processing of large corpora of phonological data, complex calculations, and other time-consuming tasks. The project could clearly not have been undertaken without some mechanization of these procedures. At the very outset of our research we therefore began developing computer programs designed to perform the most laborious parts of the project, principally the phonemic transcription of the corpora and the various statistical analyses. Our research, which began in 1960 with a study of Czech, utilized computers extensively. Machines belonging to each of the so-called three generations of computers have been used in various stages of the project. The initial analysis was performed with the aid of the IBM 650 computer. Most of the processing was done on the IBM 7070 system with the IBM 1401 used in auxiliary capacity. We also utilized the IBM System 360, Model 50, at Brown University and the IBM 1130 at Lafayette College in performing some of the final calculations. The whole project could not have made significant progress without the availability of computers and without the technical and financial aid given to us both by institutions and individuals during the various stages of the complex and expensive computer-oriented portion of our research.

Henry Kučera wishes to express his appreciation, first of all, to the John Simon H. Guggenheim Memorial Foundation and to the George A. and Eliza Gardner Howard Foundation of which he was Fellow in 1960–61. It was during this year that the original plan and the basic methodology of this research was developed and that several computer programs dealing with the Slavic languages were prepared. Henry Kučera was also aided by several subsequent grants awarded to him for his work in computational linguistics, in particular by an IBM Research Associateship at the Massachusetts Institute of Technology in 1960–63, by several summer research grants from Brown University and, in the summer of 1966, by a National Science Foundation Institutional Grant GU–1934.

George K. Monroe wishes to acknowledge the financial support of Lafayette College which made it possible for him to continue the work on the project during the summer of 1965 by awarding him a Lafayette College Faculty Summer Research Grant. To the American Council of Learned Societies goes his expression of deep gratitude for supporting his graduate studies and his research in the phonological analysis of German from 1962 to 1964 by a fellowship for advanced study in linguistics, and for continuing its support through a grant-in-aid in the summer of 1966.

Most of the computer time needed in our research was generously allocated by Brown University and the completion of our work and of this book would not have been possible without this support and without the availability of the facilities of the Brown University Computing Laboratory. Some of the final results reported here were obtained with the allocation of computer time made possible by the provisions of the National Science Foundation Facilities Grant GP–4825 awarded to Brown University.

Although almost all of the computer programs needed for the processing of the data and for the subsequent calculations were written by us, we owe our appreciation for programming advice and aid to our colleagues, students, and especially to the personnel of the Computing Laboratory of Brown University. In particular, we are grateful to Robert Staudte who assisted us with the syllable entropy program.

To our colleagues in the Department of Linguistics at Brown University also go our thanks for the many hours of stimulating discussion of our work and for numerous valuable comments. Our appreciation is due particularly to W. F. Twaddell for his aid in the analysis of German, for his careful and critical reading of the manuscript of this book, and for the additions and modifications which he suggested. The manuscript was also read and valuable comments were made by Robert H. Meskill, William Crossgrove, M. Lois Marckworth, Julie Lovins, and Ross Saunders. We are also grateful to David G. Hays, the editor of this series of publications, for his encouragement and his editorial advice, to Christine Murray for her able secretarial assistance, and to Phyllis Monroe for her help in proofreading. Although we have incorporated many of the suggestions which came to us from the various readers of the manuscript, we alone are responsible for the final formulation and for any remaining errors or shortcomings.

GEORGE K. MONROE   HENRY KUČERA
Easton, Pennsylvania   Providence, Rhode Island

November, 1967

CONTENTS

LIST OF TABLES

Chapter I

INTRODUCTION

This volume describes the procedures and the results of a quantitative comparison of syllabic structures and of phonemic constraints operative within the phonological syllable in three languages, Russian, Czech, and German. Also included is a discussion of an experimental analysis of the degrees of overall phonological "similarity" of the three languages and an investigation of the qualitative and quantitative factors accounting for such a similarity.

Some of the basic methods of the mathematical theory of communication as well as related mathematical procedures have been used in the research summarized here. The project was undertaken to test the usefulness of well-defined quantitative procedures in phonological analysis, especially in comparative and typological studies. An evaluation of the results and some suggestions for further applicability of our methods are contained in Chapter 8.

There was a dual motivation which brought us to this research: our interest in phonological typology and the possibility of exploring new methods of historical linguistics.

From our previous studies of phonology emerged the realization that the introduction of rigorous quantitative approaches was potentially productive in this area of linguistics. This seemed especially true of phonological typology, the relatively unexplored field of comparative study of the phonological structures of languages. In the past, phonological typology was mostly limited to non-quantitative analyses, and when quantitative considerations were introduced they were usually quite elementary. Most past typological studies were concerned with the comparison and classification of phonemic inventories and, at the very most, with the comparison of the organization of phonemes in terms of articulatory oppositions or distinctive features, and of general patterning of the phoneme sets. Such comparative studies of phonemic systems are certainly of value. But they can also be misleading if not supplemented by consideration of other factors. It is self-evident, for example, that two languages may have very similar or even identical inventories of phonemes,[1] differentiated by the same distinctive

---

[1] The question of the "existence" of phonemes, which has been raised by some adherents of the transformationalist school, will be discussed briefly in Chapter 3.

features, and can still be far apart in distributional and combinatory aspects of their phonologies. Consequently, phoneme strings in two such languages may be quite unlike in organization. Aside from phonotactics, quantitative factors need to be considered, such as the relative frequency of individual phonemes and phoneme strings, probabilistic constraints on the occurrence of phonemes in specified positions in relevant linguistic segments (such as syllables or words), or restrictions on sequences of larger phonological units.

A brief illustration from the analysis of the phonological data used in the preparation of this monograph may clarify this point.

In the Russian and the Czech phonological systems, the status of affricates is practically identical. In both languages, there are two affricates, /c/ and /č/, specifiable by the same distinctive features. The Russian and the Czech affricates are comparable also in their distributional properties if these are described non-quantitatively. However, a comparison of the relative frequencies of these phonemes in the two languages shows substantial differences. In Russian, the mean frequency, per 1,000 phoneme occurrences, of /c/ is 5.62, and of /č/ is 16.33. In Czech, the order of magnitude of the frequencies of the affricates is reversed; that of /c/ is 13.69, while that of /č/ is 9.91.

In the actual speech chain, therefore, the relative phonological roles of the two affricates will differ considerably between Russian and Czech.

In this particular case, a diachronic explanation of these synchronic observations is readily available. The current difference in the relative frequencies of occurrence of affricates can be explained largely as a consequence of slightly divergent phonetic changes which took place in the several groups of Slavic languages after the 6th century A.D.

Aside from contributing to the adequacy of the phonological description, such a quantitative analysis as illustrated in the quite elementary example above can indicate the extent of the effect which divergent historical phonetic changes have in the synchronic comparison of two genetically related languages. It is even conceivable that other quantitative facts of this nature may furnish clues to less well-understood diachronic developments.

The above illustration thus also points out the other motivation for our research, the desire to explore, at least in a preliminary way, the possibilities of new methodological directions in historical phonology. The notion of regular phonological correspondences and of the substantial regularity of phonetic change is the *sine qua non* of historical linguistics, and has made it possible to advance the notion of genetic relationships of languages and of the reconstructions of earlier undocumented stages of a language. These principles of historical phonology imply some basic assumptions about the stability of certain levels of language in diachronic developments.

It is well known that the morphology of a language, for example, may undergo such drastic changes in a relatively short time that the new form of the language bears only a remote similarity to the older stage. If we had no past written records and no principles of historical phonology, it would probably be impossible to make any meaningful statements about the genetic relationship of English and Russian on the basis of morphology or syntax alone. The fact that morphological patterns and types are not very durable features in the diachronic profile of a language becomes all the more obvious in a comparison of the various typological classifications of languages on the one hand and of their genetic classifications on the other. The two groupings are very frequently quite dissimilar.

The importance of historical phonology as a method for determining the genetic relationship of languages is thus based on the assumption that a significant number of phonologically different but similarly patterned strings will continue, over long periods of time, to designate identical or similar semantic concepts in genetically related languages. This basic assumption, together with the observation that phonetic change is substantially regular, makes it then possible to compare corresponding forms in two languages and make reasonable conclusions about the relationship of the languages.

The interest in historical phonology brought us thus to the question of whether the degree of similarity of phonological patterning of comparable linguistic units (such as syllables or words) in two or more languages reflects the degree of the genetic relationship of these languages and whether this degree of similarity is measurable. Henry Kučera attempted to answer this question, in a preliminary way, in a previous study (Kučera, 1964) and proposed a mathematical procedure, a so-called Isotopy Index, for the measurement of such similarity. This method is further elaborated upon and applied to the relationship among Russian, Czech, and German in Chapter 6 of this book.

Aside from the Isotopy Index calculations, the basic mathematical procedure which we followed in the quantitative phonological analysis was the application of some fairly elementary concepts of information theory.

Information theory has had a rather spotty fortune in linguistic research. Shortly after Shannon formulated his mathematical theory of communication, many linguists hailed it as capable of making an important contribution to the investigation of natural languages. Nevertheless, the applications of the method to significant linguistic problems have been few. As the center of attention of American linguistics shifted, in the late 1950's and early 1960's, to formal syntactic models of language, interest in information theory among linguists seems to have lessened considerably. This was, at least partly, a consequence of the fact that such finite state models as those offered by information theory are not suitable to serve as syntactic models of language and are, therefore, inadequate as a basis of a general linguistic theory. (See, for example, Chomsky, 1957a.)

On subsyntactic levels of linguistic analysis, however, finite state models have a potential usefulness in the description of the structure of linguistic elements. Since such units as morphemes or syllables are finite in length (i.e. are specifiable as sequences of a definite number of digital items) finite state models are in principle applicable in their analysis. The structure of the phonological syllable, for example, can be adequately and revealingly described by specifying which phonemes can occur in any given state in a sequential generation of the syllable and by enumerating all the possible states of the systems in such syllable generation.

The quantitative comparison of syllabic structure of the three languages described in this study essentially amounts to an overall determination of the sequences of phonemes which are admissible within a syllable and of the relative exploitation of such possible phonemic sequences (syllables) in actual speech. In other words, the degree of freedom with which the phonemes of the language can follow each other within the boundaries of a phonological syllable (or, in inverse terms, the number of constraints on admissible phonemic sequences within such boundaries) is being measured, together with the relative utilization of such admissible sequences in utterance formation. If the occurrence probability of syllables in speech can be estimated, the average entropy per phoneme and the redundancy of the system can be calculated for the syllables of the language. The detailed procedures of this calculation are described in Chapter 5.

Although information theory methods have been used by linguists previously, our research differs from such previous applications in a number of ways, most significantly in the selection of the unit of analysis. In our study, this unit (that is, the portion of the utterance considered as an independent event) is a functional linguistic element, the phonological syllable, which is a string of variable length. In previous studies, average entropy per phoneme was either calculated solely from probabilities of individual phonemes (so-called first-order approximations, with phonemes considered to be independent events, which is not a very revealing procedure) or for phoneme sequences of fixed length (e.g. two phoneme sequences or three phoneme sequences) with little consideration given to whether such strings coincided with functional linguistic boundaries or occurred across such boundaries.

It should be said immediately, however, that not even our method, which does make it possible to estimate the "efficiency" of syllable structuring, constitutes a determination of the overall entropy of the language. The analysis employed here treats syllables as if they were independent events and does not take into consideration the restrictions which govern the sequencing of entire syllables in the organization of larger linguistic units. It is quite possible that those languages which show a higher entropy within syllable boundaries would offset such higher values by a greater redundancy if sequences of syllables were included in the calculations.

In order to suggest at least some aspects of the constraints to which sequences of syllables are subject, Chapter 7 gives a partial analysis of the syllable composition of microsegments of our Russian corpus.

The three languages analyzed in this book were selected both for practical and for theoretical reasons. They were within the fields of primary interest and competence of the authors and appeared reasonably suitable for automatic phonemic transcription which made it possible to obtain the necessary body of phonemic data economically. From the theoretical point of view, it was thought potentially useful to analyze two languages which are genetically closely related and one which is more distantly related to them, in order to gain some indication of the extent to which the degree of genetic relationship might be reflected in the quantitative results. Moreover, it was considered to be of some interest for future research of this kind to have an indication whether highly inflected languages, as Russian and Czech are, will significantly differ in syllabic entropy values from the less inflected German. Our results contain at least partial answers to these questions which certainly need further investigation.

We have attempted to organize the book in such a manner that the reader can get the needed exposition of the linguistic concepts, terms, and procedures used in our research before he is presented with the details of our quantitative approach and with the results and interpretation of the quantitative analysis. An explanation of the procedures employed in the automatic processing of our linguistic data is given in Chapter 2. Chapters 3 and 4 are devoted to the linguistic prerequisites of the research, to the phonemic systems, and to the delimitation of the phonological syllable. The quantitative analysis and its results are described in Chapters 5 and 6, while Chapter 7 contains an extension of the discussion to segments larger than the syllable. An interpretative summary of the results is given in Chapter 8.

AUTOMATIC PHONEMIC
TRANSCRIPTION OF THE DATA

The phonemic analysis and transcription of three relatively large corpora was the first prerequisite for the informational analysis. Since the manual phonemic transcription of a significant body of data in three languages would have been overly time-consuming, the initial part of our project was the development of automatic phonemic transcription procedures to be performed by digital computers. The input for the mechanized transcription consisted of data in graphic form, recorded in conventional orthography on punched cards.

The transcription of the Russian and of the Czech input was designed in such a way that the phonemically rendered corpora would contain exactly 100,000 phonemes for each language. In the case of German, whose transcription presented special problems and required a somewhat different approach, the transcribed text contained 105,174 phonemes.

The samples constituting the corpora were selected, in all cases, from representative printed texts, all taken from twentieth-century authors. No effort was made to choose samples in the three languages which would be translations of each other, but the general character of the three corpora was comparable. Approximately 60 percent of the data for each language came from prose fiction, 20 percent from journalistic prose, 10 percent from poetry, and 10 percent from scholarly and scientific publication. The data were punched onto cards on a regular IBM 026 keypunch in standard orthography, with numerals and some special characters used for those graphemes for which there were no alphabetical characters available on the keypunch. Suprasegmental graphemes, for example capitals and italics, were not distinguished by separate codes. The Russian text was punched in transliteration in Roman characters.

The first task in the project was to achieve a correct phonemic transcription of the orthographic input. For Russian and for Czech, this phonemic transcription was performed automatically by constructing an algorithm for the transformation of the graphic representation into the respective phonemic representation. Computer programs for the IBM 650 and later for the IBM 7070 data processing systems based on these algorithms were prepared by Henry Kučera in the available assembly programming languages. While the final phonemic transcription procedure was completely automatic, some pre-editing of the text was necessary before the programs could be relied upon to work correctly in all instances. This pre-editing included primarily the indication of certain word and morpheme boundaries (referred to subsequently as disjunctures and defined in Chapter 4) which are not discernible from the graphic representation but whose identification is, in some instances, essential for the correct phonemic interpretation of the Russian and Czech graphic systems.

In Russian, the placement of word stress had to be marked in the graphic input as well. It may be theoretically possible to determine the placement of stress in Russian automatically but — if this is indeed feasible — it would require not only access to a large dictionary to determine the basic placement of stress but also complicated sets of rules to handle the shift of stress in various inflected forms of certain words. Since our primary aim at this stage of the project was to have sufficiently large corpora of phonemically transcribed data available for further analysis, we chose the rather speedy and relatively easy procedure of pre-editing Russian stress. Stress was marked by an asterisk (*), immediately following the vowel grapheme.

While the algorithm for the transcription of the Russian input was much more complex than in the case of Czech, the two transcription systems were essentially similar. The text was punched continuously on consecutive cards and the input cards were read into computer memory and analyzed sequentially. Such a sequential processing was necessary because the determination of the phonemic value of certain graphemes frequently involved, in both Slavic languages, consideration of the graphic environment not only within one graphic word but often also across graphic word boundaries. This problem is due, essentially, to the fact that in the Slavic languages the phonological structure of a word may affect the distribution of phonemes at the end of the preceding word. A phonological influence thus may be exercised across word boundaries or prepositional boundaries, both of which are represented by a blank (i.e. as a graphic word boundary) in the conventional orthographic representation.

The Russian and the Czech transcription programs scanned the input from left to right. If a grapheme was encountered which had an unambiguous phoneme equivalent, the corresponding phoneme was entered into the output area. Frequently, however, the phonemic value of a grapheme could not be determined without considering the graphic environment both to the right and to the left of the analyzed symbol. In such a case, the program first proceeded to investigate as many graphemes to the right as was necessary to resolve the ambiguity. Theoretically, at least, provisions had to be made to consider as many as nine symbols to the right; such cases were handled mainly by recursive programming procedures which made these complex situations manageable.

When the accurate determination of the phonemic value of a grapheme required the consideration of the environment to the left of the analyzed symbol, the program did not scan backwards but rather interrogated the applicable electronic switches which had been set previously when the left-hand symbols were being analyzed. Thus, the analysis of a grapheme had to determine not only its correct phonemic value but had to anticipate as well the various possible kinds of effect which the grapheme might have on the interpretation of subsequent symbols to the right of it and to set the necessary electronic switches to handle such contingencies.

The transcription system for Czech was simpler than the Russian one and was therefore attempted first, initially on the IBM 650 computer and eventually with the aid of the IBM 7070 data processing system.

Vowel phonemes presented only minor problems in the transcription of Czech. In several instances, the vowel letters of the Czech graphic system are not in a one-to-one correspondence with the vowel phonemes. None of these cases, however, was particularly difficult to handle. For example, the fact that the phoneme /i/ can be represented graphically by either *i* or *y* and, similarly, /i:/ by either *i* or *ý* presented only trivial programming problems. Signalling of consonant quality by means of the following vowel grapheme also posed a relatively easy task. For example, an algorithm was required for interpreting correctly the graphemes *t*, *d*, and *n* when they occur directly before *i* or *ě*. Normally, the graphemes *t*, *d*, and *n* designate the dental stops /t/, /d/ and the dental nasal /n/ respectively. If followed directly by *i* or *ě*, however, they designate the palatal stops /ť/, /ď/, and the palatal nasal /ņ/ respectively. Each time that *t*, *d*, or *n* were encountered, therefore, the string had to be scanned further to determine whether the following symbol was one of the vowel graphemes which signal the palatal quality of the preceding consonant and, if so, the necessary adjustment in the transcription had to be made.

The principal complication of the Czech transcription was the correct handling of voiced and voiceless consonants in certain environments. This difficulty is essentially due to the fact that, in many instances, the Czech orthography calls for the representation of voiced and voiceless consonants according to morphophonemic and, sometimes, etymological criteria, rather than phonemically. It was in such instances that the graphic environment of the analyzed symbol had to be examined to determine the correct phonemic transcription of the consonant.

The rules affecting the distribution of voiced and voiceless obstruents[2] before external disjuncture — which coincides, for the most part, with the graphic word boundary (see Chapter 4 for a detailed explanation) — depend on context specification. In normal allegro speech, the final obstruent before external disjuncture is voiced if the disjuncture is directly followed by a voiced obstruent, by the voiced allophone of /ř/, or by /v/ plus voiced obstruent. In all other cases, only voiceless obstruents occur before external disjuncture. In the Czech spelling, however, the signalling of voiced and voiceless obstruents in final word-position is generally governed by morphophonemic principles. An automatic transcription procedure thus has to apply the context rules to the graphic input in order to generate the correct phonemic interpretation. The following Czech examples illustrate this point. The situation in Russian is very similar.

Graphic representation

Phonemic representation
(/+/ is the symbol for external disjuncture)

kus dřeva	'a piece of wood'	/kuz+ dřeva/
kus řízku	'a piece of cutlet'	/kuz+ ři:sku/
kus vdolku	'a piece of pancake'	/kuz+ vdolku/
kus ledu	'a piece of ice'	/kus+ ledu/
kus chleba	'a piece of bread'	/kus+ xleba/
kus olova	'a piece of lead'	/kus+ olova/

As these examples show, the program has to scan the graphic input across a word boundary and consider the graphemes which follow the word-separation blank before the correct phonemic transcription of the final *s* in *kus* can be achieved. The situation can be even more complicated by the fact that the segment after external disjuncture may begin with a consonant cluster. A particular consonant cluster in Czech (and in Russian) may not contain both voiced and voiceless obstruents (/v/ being the exception). The last obstruent in the cluster determines whether the preceding obstruents

---

[2] The class of obstruents includes stops, fricatives, and affricates. Liquids and nasals belong to the class of sonorants.

are voiced or voiceless. Since here, too, spelling is not necessarily phonemic (but may be etymologically motivated, for example), the phonemic interpretation of the whole cluster is required before the first obstruent of the cluster can be specified as a voiced or a voiceless phoneme. In automatic phonemic transcription, certain word-final graphemes thus cannot be interpreted phonemically until the initial cluster of the following word has been analyzed. Since prepositions and prefixes are also affected by such cluster rules, the complete algorithm is fairly complicated.

For example, the graphic *část zprávy* 'a part of the message' is phonemically /ča: st+ spra: vi/. The phonemic value of the word-final *st* cannot be definitely determined until the initial cluster of *zprávy* has been interpreted as voiceless, i.e. as /sp/.

Examples such as these illustrate some problems of automatic phonemic transcription which are common to Czech and Russian, with only minor variations between the two languages. Other details of the Czech transcription program have been described previously (Kučera, 1963a).

The Russian transcription system, although it operated basically in the same manner as the Czech one, presented substantially greater difficulties. In addition to the problem of the correct determination of voiced and voiceless consonants, similar to the Czech situation, the two major complications in Russian were the interpretation of palatalized and non-palatalized consonants and the correct transcription of unstressed vowels. The two problems are to some extent interconnected. The palatalization of consonants is frequently signalled in Russian by the following vowel grapheme, not by any special symbol for the consonant itself. Thus, even in the simplest cases, the program had to scan the environment to the right every time a consonant was encountered to determine whether one of the "palatalizing" vowel graphemes was present. Moreover, to further complicate the problem, some Russian consonants are palatalized within certain clusters before other palatalized consonants. This type of "dependent" palatalization is not signalled in the orthography at all but has to be deduced from the status of the last consonant of the cluster. The rules for "dependent" palatalization are complicated and apply, in somewhat different ways, to clusters within words as well as to clusters across prepositional and prefix boundaries. A complex algorithm was thus required for the correct handling of these situations.

The second major source of difficulty stemmed from the fact that unstressed vowels in Russian orthography are rendered morphophonemically, i.e. in terms of the structure of the basic morpheme form which underlies the string, rather than in terms of the actual phonemic realization of the string. So, for example, the graphic *vodá* 'water' (with the accent on the second syllable) is phonemically /vadá/ but the graphic *vódy* 'waters' (with the accent on the first syllable) is phonemically /vódi/, and the diminutive *vódka* 'vodka' is phonemically /vótka/. This last example, by the way, also illustrates the necessity of interpreting the grapheme *d* as the phoneme /t/ in the cluster *dk*.

An even more complex situation arises when the unstressed vowel also signals palatalization of the preceding consonant. For example, the singular *délo* 'affair' is phonemically /d'éla/, but the plural is *delá* /d'ilá/. The stressed grapheme *e* of the singular form signals palatalization of the preceding *d* as well as the phoneme /é/; on the other hand, the final *o* of the singular form designates the unstressed /a/. In the plural form, *e* signals palatalization of the preceding *d* as well as the unstressed phoneme /i/; the final *a* then signals a stressed /á/. These are rather elementary examples of a complicated problem which must be faced in the automatic transcription of Russian. In some sense, it resembles the difficulty encountered in any attempt to transcribe English automatically, when formulating rules which would give the correct phonological values for *e*, *o*, and *a* in such words as *democrat*, *democracy* and *democratic*. All three words are spelled with the same three vowel graphemes but have different stress placements which then affect the phonological interpretations of the respective vowels.

In dealing with the Czech and Russian input, it was considered desirable and advantageous to perform certain statistical counts simultaneously with the transcription. Both programs counted the frequency of occurrence of all individual phonemes for every 1000 phoneme occurrences of the transcribed corpus, and also constructed a table of all phoneme digrams encountered in the analysis and counted the frequency of digrams in consecutive blocks of 10,000 running phonemes.

The phonemic transcription was written on magnetic tape in a coded form; the programs also contained an option to print the transcription on an on-line printer for proofreading and checking purposes. The results of the statistical counts could be stored either on magnetic tape or punched on cards. The execution speed of the transcription programs was quite satisfactory. With all the options in operation (i.e. simultaneous printing of the phonemic output and punching of statistical results), the transcription of Russian (which was slower) proceeded at an average speed of approximately 1000 phonemes transcribed and counted per minute.

The German data were also punched on cards in standard orthography.

Substitutions were made for the various graphic features of German which are not represented on standard IBM equipment. For example, umlaut was represented by an asterisk (*) punched immediately after the vowel to be altered, and the figure eight (8), was used in place of German 'ess-tset' (β). Citations from foreign languages and formulas were replaced by parentheses and were not considered further in the phonological analysis.

Before the German text was punched, it was pre-edited. By this process, prefixes, both separable and inseparable, were separated from the stem by a hyphen, e.g. *begann* as BE-GANN, *Anstrengungen* as AN-STRENGUNGEN, *aufgebaut* as AUF-GE-BAUT. Second, elements of compounds were separated by a slash line, e.g. *Lobgesang* as LOB/GE-SANG.

The problems in the phonemic transcription of the German texts were of a somewhat different nature than in the Slavic languages. It quickly became apparent that any algorithm for a completely automatic phonemic transcription of a German graphic input would have to rely on such an extensive dictionary look-up procedure that the necessary computer programs would be quite complicated and cumbersome. This problem is due to those characteristics of the German orthography which frequently make the phonemic value of graphemes and combinations of graphemes ambiguous, even when a relatively large environment of the analyzed symbol is taken into consideration. The problem is particularly troublesome with regard to the correct determination of the length of vocalic phonemes. At the same time, however, it was apparent that — unlike that of Russian and Czech — the phonemic transcription of the German texts does not need to involve the consideration of the environment beyond the graphic word boundaries. For these reasons, an expedient semi-automatic transcription procedure was adopted for German by George K. Monroe. It consisted of several computer programs which, initially, segmented the running text into graphic words, sorted these words alphabetically and merged identical entries, keeping track of the frequency of occurrence of each such graphic word, and then performed a tentative phonemic transcription of each graphic word separately. This approach saved a great deal of processing time because the algorithm for phonemic transcription of any word, including a very frequent one, had to be applied only once in the processing of the whole German corpus.

The results of the tentative phonemic transcription of the German words were punched on an on-line card punch. The initial transcription program was so written that dubious transcriptions were automatically identified in the output by a special symbol. These tentative transcriptions were inspected and the errors were corrected manually. The corrected transcription, which also contained the necessary statistical information about the occurrence frequency of individual words, was then written on magnetic tape.

Subsequent computer programs used the phonemic transcriptions on magnetic tapes as input. These programs incorporated algorithms for the analysis of the phonemic strings into phonological syllables (in accordance with principles described in Chapter 4), and also contained instructions for generating tables for all syllables found in the three corpora as well as for estimating the occurrence probability of each syllable. The computation of entropy and redundancy of the phonological syllables in Russian, Czech and German was accomplished with the aid of Fortran and assembly language programs for the IBM 7070 and IBM 360 systems.

Chapter 3

PHONOLOGICAL ANALYSIS—SEGMENTAL PHONEMES

In order to achieve as generally valid a description of the phonological properties of the three languages as possible, we decided not to base the phonemic transcription on the idiolects of particular speakers but rather to attempt to achieve transcriptions representing the "standard" phonological forms of the languages. This made it necessary, first of all, to select the "standard" form of each of the three languages and to determine the phonological properties of these codes. Fortunately, the notion of a "standard" or "literary" form is well established in all three languages which we were investigating, and usable analyses and descriptions of the phonological properties of these codes are available. But even with the availability of previous studies, many problems remained. The inconsistencies and differences between alternate phonological descriptions had to be reconciled and many detailed decisions about the "standard" phonemic realization of various grapheme combinations and strings had to be made. But had we had to deal with English, for example, in which the notion of a standard phonological form of the language is not so well established, our problems would have doubtless been much greater.

Since our interest was a comparative study of the utilization of phonological elements in actual utterances (rather than in the lexicon), we were concerned with certain aspects of linguistic performance. Perhaps a few words need to be said about this point.

In the comparative analysis reported here, we have attempted to examine not only the composition of the phonological syllables in the three languages but also the relative exploitation of the different syllabic structures in speech. This approach has made it possible to formulate some linguistically relevant generalizations about the functional utilization of syllables of various types in the communication process but, of course, also required the analysis of actual utterances. In addition to this, the rationale of our determination of the parameters of phonological similarity among the three languages and of the correlation of the components of this similarity with the genetic relationship of languages (explained in Chapter 6) is dependent on taking the relative frequency of occurrence of the phonological elements into account. Thus, the aims of our research required the phonological analysis of sets of utterances rather than of individual lexicons.

The concept and the definition of a *phoneme* vary considerably among various linguistic schools. Some adherents of the linguistic theory of "transformational grammar" have denied the existence of a separate phonemic level in the structure of language, while Chomsky has recently stated, somewhat more cautiously, that "the status of the concept 'phoneme' is very much in doubt" (Chomsky, 1966, p. 45).

Regardless of disagreements among phonologists, there can be little doubt about some basic facts: first, that humans encode and decode linguistic messages as sequences of discrete phonological segments, not as an acoustic continuum; and second, that the various phonological segments of speech — no two of which are acoustically identical — are grouped into a rather small set of functionally relevant classes according to a few distinctive properties which such sounds share. It is useful to call each such class of sounds a "phoneme". How exactly the segmentation of speech into discrete units is performed, and which phonetic and grammatical factors play a role in the grouping of sounds into phoneme classes, still remains to be investigated. But as Householder has pointed out, the function of phonemes as conceived by the linguistic pioneers of the thirties and forties "was to explain the manner in which speakers can *repeat* (not just *mimic*) new words" (Householder, 1966, p. 99). This kind of ability, exercisable even in the absence of any indicators of meaning or of grammatical function of the new word, clearly points to the speaker's systematic analysis of the sound pattern of his language without any necessary reference to deep morphophonemic potential and without the requirement of imitation of all the minute phonetic detail in the reproduced item.

The functional grouping of the indeterminate number of different sounds into a small set of phoneme classes makes it possible to investigate the phonological structuring of languages and to reach some conclusions about the statistical properties of speech on the phonological level.

The basic assumption of the existence of a distinct phonemic level of language and, consequently, the question of the possibility of identifying phonemes and delimiting phonological syllables depends to a large extent on the linguistic theory which one adopts.

In a process description of language, such as that used in transformational grammar, the actual language structures are accounted for by deriving one linguistic entity from another by means of rewrite rules. Such rules are ordered and there are certain limitations on the number and nature of elements which may be rewritten by a single rule. Nevertheless, there is generally no requirement in process grammars that rules appropriate to specific levels of language must not be interspersed with rules of another level. So, for example, there is no requirement in the phonological theory of transformational grammar that *all* rules which pertain to the "systematic phonemic" representation must precede *all* rules producing the "systematic phonetic" representation or, in other words, it is not necessary that all the phonological statements based on classificatory distinctive features precede the mapping of the classificatory matrix into an output specified in terms of a universal phonemic alphabet (for a detailed discussion see Kučera, 1967). As a consequence, a process grammar makes it difficult or impossible to identify the separate strata of language. A linguistic theory committed to a process description obscures and, in the final analysis, denies the concept of language as a system of systems, i.e. the notion of language as a hierarchically organized structure of interdependent strata, with each stratum having an inventory of categories or elements (i.e. an alphabet) and a set of combinatory rules for organizing these units (i.e. tactics).

In our opinion, the negation of the structure of language as a system of systems is a serious shortcoming of transformational linguistic theory. Without subscribing to "stratificational grammar" in the technical sense (i.e. to the theory of language as formulated for example by Lamb, 1966 a and b), our method assumes the existence of an identifiable phonological stratum with a finite inventory of elements (phonemes) and the tactics which determine the combinations of phonemes in phonological syllables.

In all three languages analyzed in this monograph, the inventory of segmental phonemes was determined by making use of the distinctive feature approach of Jakobson *et al.* The Jakobsonian methodology essentially proceeds from the identification of those phonological oppositions (or features) which are distinctive in the given language, that is, those which can signal distinctions between strings with different meanings. A feature may refer either to the presence or the absence of a phonological quality (e.g. nasal *vs.* non-nasal, voiced or voiceless) or to two polar manifestations of a phonological quality (e.g. grave *vs.* acute). Consequently, some of the distinctive features are defined in relative, not in absolute terms. This means that the feature values for a given phoneme must be determined, in such instances, in relation to a class of phonemes to which the given phoneme is assigned in the system. This, of course, also makes it conceivable that acoustically similar classes of sounds in two languages could have different feature specifications, as determined by the overall structure of each system.[3]

A bundle of distinctive features specifies a phoneme, which can thus be considered to be a class of sounds differentiated from all other sounds of the language by the same set of distinctive oppositions. The submembers or allophones of a phoneme are those sounds which are specified by the same set of distinctive feature values.

A feature which is distinctive in one language may not be utilized at all in another language or may simply serve in the role of a redundant (i.e. predictable) feature. For example, the opposition between palatalized and non-palatalized consonants is distinctive in Russian, but not utilized in Czech and in German. On the other hand, the opposition between long and short vowels is distinctive in Czech and in German. In Russian, differences in vowel length also exist but such differences are predictable in terms of the placement of stress, with the longer vowels generally occurring under stress. The feature long vs. short is therefore redundant in Russian and need not be included at all in the feature matrix.

Even within the same language, a distinctive feature may be applicable to certain phonological segments only. In both Russian and Czech, for example, the feature voiced vs. voiceless differentiates two large sets of consonants. In the affricates /c/ and /č/, however, the voiced vs. voiceless feature is redundant. Affricates in both languages can be voiced or voiceless, as determined by different phonological environments.

The segmental phonemes for each of the three languages are displayed in distinctive feature Tables 1, 2, and 3. These tables follow the usual notational convention. The plus sign in a column indicates that the first quality in the respective row characterizes the phoneme in question; conversely, a minus sign indicates that the second quality of the listed opposition applies to the particular phoneme; and a zero shows that the feature specification for the phoneme in that column is unnecessary.

It should be pointed out that the zero symbol in the feature matrix represents either a plus or a minus sign which can be supplied by a redundancy rule. The logic is thus not three-valued; the phonological description operates only with a binary set of symbols, plus and minus. There are, however, three types of redundancy rules and thus three "types" of zeros:

a) A zero representing a plus or a minus quality which is universally redundant and can thus be supplied by a rule applicable to all languages.

---

[3] For a more detailed discussion of this aspect of distinctive features, see Chomsky's review of Jakobson's and Halle's *Fundamentals of Language* (Chomsky, 1957c).

Halle gives an example of such a situation for consonants: "Since all *compact* consonants are *non-diffuse* and all *diffuse* consonants, *non-compact*, only one of the two features functions distinctively in the consonants. We therefore describe labials and dentals as *non-compact*; palatals, velars, gutturals, etc. as *compact*, and omit reference to feature *diffuse–non-diffuse*" (Halle, 1957, p. 71).

b) A zero representing a plus or a minus quality predictable for a specific language (but not universally) by a rule which refers only to other features specified for the given segment but not to other segments in the string. Since all vowels (i.e. vocalic non-consonantal segments) in standard Russian, Czech, and German are normally non-nasal, the zeros in the vowel columns for the nasal *vs.* non-nasal feature rows can be replaced by a minus with this type of rule, in all three languages.

c) A zero representing a plus or a minus, predictable for a specific language, but only if the phonological environment is taken into account, i.e. if reference is made to other segments in the string or to boundaries. For example, the voiced or voiceless quality of the Rusian and Czech /c/ or /č/ can be predicted by a rule of this kind which must refer to neighboring phonemes or disjunctures.[4]

3.1. The Segmental Phonemes of Czech

Establishing the set of segmental phonemes for Czech and preparing the algorithm for the mechanical transcription of the Czech input was easier than in the other two languages analyzed in our project. This was due, first of all, to the fact that the standard code, or "literary language" — as it is known in Czech usage — is a well-codified form whose phonological structure does not present major difficulties. In part, at least, this high degree of codi-fication is the result of historical circumstances. Present-day standard Czech, as far as its phonology is concerned, is to some extent an artificial code which does not completely coincide with the phonological structure of any of the Czech dialects. The modern standard language is the product of the Czech National Revival, a cultural and political emancipation movement of considerable force which took place in Bohemia and Moravia at the end of the 18th and at the beginning of the 19th centuries. One task which this national movement set for itself was the reestablishment of a standard Czech language for literary, scholarly and journalistic purposes. Since the orientation of the National Revival was historical, with the more glorious past of the nation

---

4 Several aspects of the logical basis of the distinctive feature theory are discussed in a recent article by R. D. Wilson (1966).

serving as inspiration for the national resurrection, a number of archaic phonological features — long before altered by historical changes in the Czech dialects — were preserved in the phonology of the reestablished standard language and have persisted in it, with only minor exceptions, ever since.

The standard language, on which this analysis is based, is taught in schools, used in the mass media of communication, employed in most writing and in print (with the occasional exception of fiction in which the colloquial language may be utilized sporadically for artistic purposes), and is extensively used as a spoken language in public speeches, sermons, and other official and formal communications. Interestingly enough, in conversations of an informal nature, among friends, members of the family, and frequently even under very general circumstances, a non-standard colloquial variety of Czech is used by most speakers of Czech, even well-educated ones who are thoroughly familiar with the standard code. This colloquial language is phonologically somewhat different from the standard form, both in its inventory of segmental phonemes and in distributional properties of phonemes. These differences are described in detail in *The Phonology of Czech* (Kučera, 1961). None of the phonological peculiarities of the colloquial language are reflected in the analysis reported here.

Although the basic phonological structure of Czech did not present major problems, the transcription algorithm was not without difficulties. These concerned primarily subtleties which are usually ignored in the various descriptions of the standard language and in manuals of "standard pronunciation" but which must be specified in any computer processing of data, where all parts of the task have to be made explicit. Among such problems were, for example, exact rules for determining the voiced or voiceless quality of a final consonant or of a consonantal cluster when it is followed, without pause, by a word beginning also with a consonant. The manuals of standard pronunciation published in Czechoslovakia give only scanty information about such situations and we had to rely on the recordings of the standard speech of a number of Czech speakers in reaching adequate solutions (cf. Kučera, 1961, pp. 94 ff). But the very existence of this difficulty was instructive by demonstrating again that the explicitness required in computer processing can have the beneficial effect of forcing a more rigorous and complete statement of the linguistic problem itself.

Another complication was the treatment of those loan words whose pronunciation deviates from the general rules applicable in indigenous words. This problem was solved mostly by pre-editing, which was not very cumbersome because of the relatively sparse occurrence of such loans.

The introduction of phrase boundaries in the pre-editing of the text proved necessary (as it did in Russian) because the presence or absence of a phrase boundary (redefined in Chapter 4 as *terminal disjuncture*) affects the distribution, in both Czech and Russian, of certain voiced and voiceless consonants. The phrase boundary is manifested in normal speech as a brief pause; its introduction is to some extent optional and depends on speech tempo, the organization of emphatic stress in the sentence, and on other partially subjective factors. Since only printed texts were used for the phonemic transcription in this project, the introduction of a phrase boundary, where it was not clearly marked by punctuation, was to some extent a matter of subjective judgment. Generally speaking, the effort was made to insert phrase boundaries in those places where they could be considered as optional by assuming a "normal" speech tempo with as neutral an emphasis pattern as the meaning of the passage allowed. This procedure was followed for both Czech and Russian. Some of the quantitative results were of course affected by such subjective decisions; however, the genuinely dubious situations were few and their overall effect on the final statistical conclusions was probably insignificant.

Table 1 displays the phonemes and the distinctive feature specifications of present-day standard Czech. In our analysis, the system has 24 consonants, 10 vowels, and the semivowel /j/.

Several of the principal allophones of the phonemic system of standard Czech are the result of the predictable distribution of the feature voiced *vs.* voiceless in several consonant phonemes. Thus /c/ has the voiceless allophone [c] and the voiced allophone [ʒ]; the phoneme /č/ can be realized as [č] or as [ǯ]; and /ř/ has the voiceless allophone [ř̥] and the voiced allophone [ř̬]. This fact accounts for the zeros in the voiced *vs.* voiceless row of these segments.

The phone [γ], which is a voiced velar fricative, occurs in some idiolects and is considered acceptable in standard Czech. It is in complementary distribution with the voiceless [x] and, frequently, in free variation with the voiced [h]. In Czech phonetic descriptions, [γ] is generally considered a variant of the phoneme /x/ because of articulatory reasons (both [x] and [γ] are velar fricatives). But this is not a phonologically sound solution. In our analysis, we class [γ] as a free variant of the phoneme /h/. Both submembers of /h/, namely [h] and [γ], are then identified as non-vocalic, consonantal, compact, grave, non-nasal, continuous, and voiced.

The phoneme /n/ has two allophones, dental [n] and velar [ŋ], the latter occurring directly before /k/ or /g/. It is this allophonic situation which

Table 1.—Phonemes and distinctive features of Czech

	p	b	d	ț	ḑ	k	g	c	č	f	v	s	z	š	ž	x	h	l	r	ř	m	n	ŋ	j	i	iː	e	eː	u	uː	o	oː	a	aː
vocalic vs. non-vocalic	−	−	−	−	−	−	−	−	−	−	−	−	−	−	−	−	−	+	+	+	−	−	−	−	+	+	+	+	+	+	+	+	+	+
consonantal vs. non-cons.	+	+	+	+	+	+	+	+	+	+	+	+	+	+	+	+	+	+	+	+	+	+	+	−	−	−	−	−	−	−	−	−	−	−
compact vs. non-compact	−	−	−	+	+	+	+	−	+	−	−	−	−	+	+	+	+	0	0	0	−	−	+	+	−	−	−	−	−	−	−	−	+	+
diffuse vs. non-diffuse	+	+	+	−	−	−	−	+	−	+	+	+	+	−	−	−	−	0	0	0	+	+	−	−	+	+	−	−	+	+	−	−	−	−
grave vs. non-grave	+	+	−	−	−	+	+	−	−	+	+	−	−	−	−	+	+	0	0	0	+	−	+	−	−	−	−	−	+	+	+	+	0	0
acute vs. non-acute	0	0	0	+	+	0	0	+	+	0	0	+	+	+	+	0	0	0	0	0	0	0	0	+	+	+	+	+	0	0	0	0	0	0
long vs. short	0	0	0	0	0	0	0	0	0	0	0	0	0	0	0	0	0	0	0	0	0	0	0	0	−	+	−	+	−	+	−	+	−	+
syllabic vs. non-syllabic	0	0	0	0	0	0	0	0	0	0	0	0	0	0	0	0	0	+	+	+	0	0	0	−	+	+	+	+	+	+	+	+	+	+
nasal vs. non-nasal	−	−	−	−	−	−	−	−	−	−	−	−	−	−	−	−	−	−	−	−	+	+	+	−	0	0	0	0	0	0	0	0	0	0
continuous vs. non-cont.	−	−	−	−	−	−	−	−	−	+	+	+	+	+	+	+	+	+	−	+	−	−	−	+	0	0	0	0	0	0	0	0	0	0
voiced vs. voiceless	−	+	+	−	+	−	+	−	−	−	+	−	+	−	+	−	+	+	+	+	+	+	+	+	0	0	0	0	0	0	0	0	0	0
strident vs. mellow	0	0	−	−	−	0	0	+	+	+	+	+	+	+	+	−	−	0	−	+	0	0	0	0	0	0	0	0	0	0	0	0	0	0

requires the introduction of the feature acute *vs.* non-acute for the Czech nasals (see also Jakobson, 1957).

A detailed discussion of the segmental phoneme analysis and of the allophone distribution can be found in *The Phonology of Czech* (Kučera, 1961), which also elaborates further on the distinctive feature analysis presented in Table 1.

3.2. The Segmental Phonemes of Russian

In establishing the phonological system of the Russian standard language, the still noticeable conflict between the older "Moscow standard" and the newer, more general, standard phonological pattern had to be taken into consideration. Perhaps as recently as a quarter of a century ago, most Russian linguists still considered the "Moscow pronunciation" as the basis of the phonological system of standard Russian. But since then the situation has changed considerably and the newer, less locally limited speech patterns have been given increased prestige by such distinguished Russian phoneticians as R. I. Avanesov, in whose recent works they function as the basis of the standard phonological form of Russian. It is true that even in Avanesov's discussion of *russkoe literaturnoe proiznošenie* ("Russian literary pronunciation") a number of Moscow forms are still admitted as legitimate options (see Avanesov, 1954 and 1956, Avanesov and Ožegov, 1960). However, the trend seems quite unmistakable and the future hegemony of the newer non-Moscow standard is clearly indicated.

The "new standard" cannot be identified geographically, as the older one could, although certain characteristics of the Leningrad pronunciation are recognizable in it. The new standard has clearly been influenced by spelling pronunciation. This is certainly not surprising in a country in which literacy rates have increased dramatically in the last few decades. It must also be remembered that the Soviet Union is a multilingual country in which native Russians, strictly speaking, constitute only a little over one-half of the population. The remainder, both the Slavic speaking Ukrainians and Byelorussians, and non-Slavic nations as the Turkic peoples of Soviet Central Asia, or the Georgians and Armenians, the Baltic peoples, and the various minorities of Altaic, Uralic and other linguistic families, all have to learn, to some extent at least, Russian, the *lingua franca* of the Soviet Union. In such a mass pedagogical enterprise, any pronunciation standard which exhibits more consistent correspondences with the written form of the language has obvious advantages.

The ascendancy of the new phonological standard was, of course, welcome in our project because it reduced the number of problems in the automatic transcription of the Russian input. Whenever the authoritative descriptions of the standard language allowed two acceptable alternatives, our transcription algorithm followed the new standard, which was also invariably easier to program.

The details of Russian phonology and of the phoneme–grapheme correspondences are too numerous to be listed here; a separate monograph would be required for their thorough description. The reader interested in the principles which we followed can find them in the various works of R. I. Avanesov, especially in his comprehensive *Russkoe literaturnoe proiznošenie* (1954) and in several other works listed in the bibliography.

It may be useful, however, to give here a few examples of the differences between the older Moscow forms and the newer standard, to illustrate the nature of the differences. While, for example, the phonetic correspondent of the grapheme щ in the Moscow pronunciation is a long palatalized fricative [š':], the new standard uses here the sound combination [šč]. In the masc. nom. sg. endings of adjectives whose stem terminates in a velar consonant, such as (in transliteration) *širokij* 'wide', the Moscow standard calls for a mid-central allophone of /a/ after the velar, without any palatalization of the velar stop, i.e. for a phonemic realization /širókaj/; the new standard, clearly under the influence of spelling, now has the phonemic realization /širók'ij/. Similarly, in the Moscow pronunciation, there is a distinction between the nominative-accusative suffix and the locative suffix of soft neutral nouns; in the new standard, no such distinction is required, again in correspondence with the lack of any distinction between these suffixes in spelling.

The new standard is also more conservative in the treatment of "dependent" palatalization of consonants in clusters. Fewer consonants are now required to be palatalized in clusters before another palatalized consonant than was the case in the Moscow-based standard. This, too, can be viewed as a side effect of spelling pronunciation.

The examples listed here are not intended to be exhaustive but simply to illustrate the recent tendencies in the phonological development of standard Russian. The reader should also bear in mind that the quantitative results reported in this monograph are based on a transcription performed in accordance with the new standard and, in cases of optional forms, with a preference for the forms of the new standard.

Table 2 displays the segmental phonemes of present-day standard Russian and of their distinctive features. In our analysis, the system has a phonemic inventory of 32 consonants, 8 vowels, and the semivowel /j/.

Table 2.—Phonemes and distinctive features of Russian

	p	p′	b	b′	t	t′	d	d′	k	k′	g	c	č	f	f′	v	v′	s	s′	z	z′	š	ž	x	l	l′	r	r′	m	m′	n	n′	j	i	í	é	u	ú	ó	a	á
vocalic vs. non-vocalic	−	−	−	−	−	−	−	−	−	−	−	−	−	−	−	−	−	−	−	−	−	−	−	−	+	+	+	+	−	−	−	−	0	+	+	+	+	+	+	+	+
consonantal vs. non-cons.	+	+	+	+	+	+	+	+	+	+	+	+	+	+	+	+	+	+	+	+	+	+	+	+	+	+	+	+	+	+	+	+	−	−	−	−	−	−	−	−	−
compact vs. non-compact	−	−	−	−	−	−	−	−	+	+	+	−	+	−	−	−	−	−	−	−	−	+	+	+	−	−	−	−	−	−	−	−	0	−	−	+	−	−	+	+	+
diffuse vs. non-diffuse	+	+	+	+	+	+	+	+	−	−	−	+	−	+	+	+	+	+	+	+	+	−	−	−	0	0	0	0	+	+	+	+	0	+	+	−	+	+	−	−	−
low vs. high tonality	+	+	+	+	−	−	−	−	+	+	+	−	−	+	+	+	+	−	−	−	−	+	+	+	+	−	+	−	+	+	−	−	−	−	−	−	+	+	+	+	+
stressed vs. unstressed	0	0	0	0	0	0	0	0	0	0	0	0	0	0	0	0	0	0	0	0	0	0	0	0	0	0	0	0	0	0	0	0	0	−	+	+	−	+	+	−	+
syllabic vs. non-syllabic	0	0	0	0	0	0	0	0	0	0	0	0	0	0	0	0	0	0	0	0	0	0	0	0	0	0	0	0	0	0	0	0	−	+	+	+	+	+	+	+	+
nasal vs. non-nasal	−	−	−	−	−	−	−	−	−	−	−	−	−	−	−	−	−	−	−	−	−	−	−	−	−	−	−	−	+	+	+	+	−	0	0	0	0	0	0	0	0
continuous vs. non-continuous	−	−	−	−	−	−	−	−	−	−	−	−	−	+	+	+	+	+	+	+	+	+	+	+	+	+	+	+	−	−	−	−	+	0	0	0	0	0	0	0	0
voiced vs. voiceless	−	−	+	+	−	−	+	+	−	−	+	−	−	−	−	+	+	−	−	+	+	−	+	−	0	0	0	0	0	0	0	0	0	0	0	0	0	0	0	0	0
sharp vs. plain	−	+	−	+	−	+	−	+	−	+	0	−	+	−	+	−	+	−	+	−	+	−	−	−	−	+	−	+	−	+	−	+	+	0	0	0	0	0	0	0	0
strident vs. mellow	0	0	0	0	−	−	−	−	0	0	0	+	+	+	+	+	+	+	+	+	+	+	+	−	0	0	0	0	0	0	0	0	0	0	0	0	0	0	0	0	0

As in Czech, several major allophones of the Russian system are accounted for by the predictable distribution of the voiced *vs.* voiceless feature in certain consonants. The Russian phoneme /c/ has the voiceless variant [c] and the voiced variant [ʒ]; /č/ has the allophones [č] and [ǯ], and /x/ the voiceless allophone [x] and the voiced [ɣ]. These facts account for the zeros in the voiced *vs.* voiceless row of these phonemes.

The palatalized velar stop /k'/ is a phoneme of marginal status; it occurs in complementary distribution with the non-palatalized /k/ except in the minimal pair /satkóm/ 'fish pond' (instr. sg.) *vs.* /satk'óm/ 'let us weave it together'. No comparable minimal pair can be found in the standard language to demonstrate the phonemic contrast between the non-palatalized [g] and the palatalized [g'], although such minimal pairs do exist in non-standard speech. These two phones are thus considered in our analysis to be sub-members of the phoneme /g/. The same is true of the velar fricatives [x'] and [x]. In these cases, the palatalized and non-palatalized phones are in complementary distribution. It is this fact which accounts for the asymmetry of the Russian system in velar phonemes and which explains the zeros in the sharp *vs.* plain row for /g/ and /x/.

The feature low tonality *vs.* high tonality combines the feature grave *vs.* acute (the primary tonality feature of consonants) with the feature flat *vs.* non-flat (the tonality feature of vowels) which are in complementary distribution. Details regarding the acoustic properties of this feature in consonants and in vowels can be found in *The Sound Pattern of Russian* (Halle, 1959, pp. 53–54).

The vowel system of Russian differs from the seemingly similar Czech vowel system both with regard to prosodic features and with regard to tonality features. The Russian vowel system contains the distinctive feature stressed *vs.* unstressed, with increased vowel length being an optional manifestation of stressed vowels. In Czech, on the other hand, the feature short *vs.* long is distinctive for all vowels but the placement of stress is not, since it is predictable in terms of certain phonological boundaries (see Chapter 4 for details).

Equally important is the less obvious difference in the tonality features. In Russian, vowels are differentiated as flat *vs.* non-flat which, in articulatory terms, correlates with the opposition rounded *vs.* unrounded. In Czech, on the other hand, vowels are differentiated primarily by the feature grave *vs.* acute, for which the articulatory correlates are back *vs.* front tongue position.

This difference in features is clearly reflected in vowel allophones. In

Russian, the rounded phonemes /u/ and /o/ are realized not only as back vowels but also as front variants [ü] and [ö] respectively. It should be also noted that the phoneme /a/ has, besides a central variant, the front allophone [æ]. The fronted variants of Russian vowels, which occur in the neighborhood of palatalized consonants, clearly demonstrate that the articulatory opposition front *vs.* back does not play the primary distinctive role in the Russian vowel system. In Czech, on the other hand, no comparable fronted allophones exist and the basic front *vs.* back opposition is preserved regardless of environment. Vowel rounding in Czech is thus predictable in terms of place of articulation and can be considered to be a redundant feature. The difference between distinctive and redundant features is clearly evident in comparing the substitution sounds which Russian and Czech use in loan words for foreign front rounded vowels, such as the German or French [ü] and [ö]. Russian substitutes /u/ and /o/ respectively with a concomitant palatalization of the preceding consonant; the palatalization signals the front allophones of the rounded vowels. In Czech, on the other hand, such foreign sounds are always represented by /i/ and /e/ respectively. In Russian, the determining feature in such substitution process is the rounding (i.e. the feature flat *vs.* non-flat), in Czech the frontness (i.e. the feature grave *vs.* acute) of the foreign vowel. This accounts for such distinctions in loan words as the Russian /b'uró/ and the Czech /biro:/ 'bureau'. Since we shall eventually contrast the Russian and the Czech phonological systems with that of German (which utilizes both the features grave *vs.* acute and flat *vs.* non-flat to distinguish vowels), the difference between Russian and Czech will be a relevant consideration in this comparison.

The feature specification of /j/ presents complications. The solution adopted here would probably not be accepted by all specialists in Russian phonology, although it appears most logical to us. Halle, for example, specifies /j/ as a glide, that is as non-vocalic and non-consonantal, with other features redundant. There is serious doubt that this represents a satisfactory description. Halle himself remarks later in his book, when discussing the sonograms of /j/ and /i/: "In a great many instances it was impossible to be sure that the subject had actually uttered /j/ and not the vowel" (Halle, 1959, p. 125). The distinctive feature status of /j/ is also troublesome in Czech (see Kučera, 1961, pp. 28–29). After considering the evidence, the most realistic solution seemed to us the addition of the prosodic feature syllabic *vs.* non-syllabic to the matrix. It is only this opposition which consistently differentiates between all the variants of /i/ and /j/. The same solution has been adopted for Czech in Table 1. The details of the distinctive feature specifications do not affect the subsequent calculation of syllabic entropy because these computations are based on phonemes, not on features. However, the feature values do influence the results of the Isotopy Index, one factor of which depends on distinctive feature analysis.

3.3. The Segmental Phonemes of German

The analysis of the standard German phonological system presupposes a form of the language mutually intelligible to educated German speakers. In our study, this is taken to be standard High German as described in *Siebs Deutsche Hochsprache* (Siebs, 1961), modified only where the common practice of a large number of educated speakers indicates an established departure from the Siebs description. An account of the development and influence of the standard form of German can be found in the introduction to the various editions of the Siebs book and in Twaddell's article, "Standard German" (1959). A brief summary of this history is presented here.

There is evidence of the growth of a literary form of the German language from the 16th century on. This standardized written form, *Schriftdeutsch*, was manifested by conformity in manner of expression, in word forms, in choice of words and in orthography. In a comparative study which includes German and Czech, it is of interest to note that the early history of *Schriftdeutsch* is connected with the Imperial Chancellery of Charles IV in Prague. The language of the Imperial Chancellery in the 14th century seems to have been a faithful reflection of the local German dialect of Prague, cultivated with attention to consistency in spelling and sentence structure. The German speech of Prague belonged to the East Middle German dialect area which had linguistically favorable compromise qualities inside the general High German domain. When the Imperial Chancellery was moved from Prague to Vienna, it was the Meissen Chancellery which acquired the secondary political prestige from Prague and maintained the inherent linguistic advantages of being East Middle German. "Throughout the 16–18th centuries, an appeal to 'Meissnisch' was a claim on respect" (Twaddell, 1959, p. 3).

In spite of the unifying influence of this standardized written language, the spoken language was anything but uniform. The problem first became a matter of concern in the theater. It is easy to see the disturbing incongruity of a situation in which various actors, supposedly playing members of the same family, would speak in several different dialectal forms of German. Goethe himself recognized the problem and admonished his actors to rid themselves of dialectal peculiarities and to adopt a dialect-free form of speech.

Although the need for a standard form of speech was recognized, it was not fulfilled immediately. The strides taken in the study of language during the 19th century, however, provided the means for the establishment of a form of German which could be taken as a suitable common standard for all Germans. In 1898, Theodor Siebs published the first edition of *Deutsche Bühnenaussprache*, a guide to the pronunciation of German words to be preferred for stage use.

Siebs' book gradually asserted itself in a sphere of wider influence both because its creator was "a man of vision", as he has often been hailed in Germany, and because a need for a common spoken German became more urgent in areas other than the theater. Siebs expressed a belief in later editions of *Bühnenaussprache* that there were non-theatrical areas in which his guide could be useful, and, indeed, its use became widespread enough for its editor to change the title in 1922 to *Deutsche Hochsprache*.

There was never any intention on the part of the editors of the Siebs guide to have the recommended forms become the sole acceptable pronunciations of German words. It was agreed that the "Hochsprache" would exist side-by-side with the "Umgangssprache", the colloquial codes common to the various regional centers. The value of the Hochsprache would be its ability to be used when local forms would be disturbing, as from the speaker's platform or in church use.

The use of the Hochsprache has spread in such foreseen ways as well as in others. The advent of radio broadcasting brought a great need for a form of German which all the listeners in a large reception area could understand. This was also true of other forms of long-range voice communication. The most dramatic need for common spoken German appeared in Germany after World War II. The widespread migration of political refugees has caused the shift of sizeable portions of the population across large numbers of isoglosses. Thus, communication in the local forms of German frequently became impractical. When there was enough of a change in a community structure, the question of the form of German to be used in teaching became real. In this case, the answer was close at hand — the Hochsprache.

Thus, while the Hochsprache is in some ways an artificiality, it is the form of German having the broadest range of intelligibility. It is this form that has been chosen for the phonemic transcription of our German corpus.

The segmental phonemes of present-day standard German and their distinctive features are displayed in Table 3. Our analysis is based on the phonemic inventory of 19 consonants and 14 vowels.

Our feature matrix differs somewhat from other distinctive feature analyses

Table 3.—Phonemes and distinctive features of German

	p	b	t	d	k	g	f	v	s	z	š	ž	x	h	l	r	m	n	ŋ	i	i:	ü	ü:	e	e:	ö	ö:	u	u:	o	o:	a	a:
vocalic vs. non-vocalic	−	−	−	−	−	−	−	−	−	−	−	−	−	−	+	+	−	−	−	+	+	+	+	+	+	+	+	+	+	+	+	+	+
consonantal vs. non-cons.	+	+	+	+	+	+	+	+	+	+	+	+	+	−	+	+	+	+	+	−	−	−	−	−	−	−	−	−	−	−	−	−	−
compact vs. non-compact	−	−	−	−	+	+	−	−	−	−	+	+	+	0	−	−	−	−	+	−	−	−	−	−	−	−	−	−	−	−	−	+	+
diffuse vs. non-diffuse	+	+	+	+	−	−	+	+	+	+	−	−	−	0	+	+	+	+	−	+	+	+	+	−	−	−	−	+	+	−	−	−	−
grave vs. acute	+	+	−	−	+	+	+	+	−	−	−	−	+	0	−	+	+	−	+	−	−	−	−	−	−	−	−	+	+	+	+	+	+
long vs. short	0	0	0	0	0	0	0	0	0	0	0	0	0	0	0	0	0	0	0	−	+	−	+	−	+	−	+	−	+	−	+	−	+
flat vs. non-flat	0	0	0	0	0	0	0	0	0	0	0	0	0	0	0	0	0	0	0	−	−	+	+	−	−	+	+	+	+	+	+	−	−
nasal vs. non-nasal	−	−	−	−	−	−	−	−	−	−	−	−	−	−	−	−	+	+	+	0	0	0	0	0	0	0	0	0	0	0	0	0	0
continuous vs. non-cont.	−	−	−	−	−	−	+	+	+	+	+	+	+	+	+	+	0	0	0	0	0	0	0	0	0	0	0	0	0	0	0	0	0
voiced vs. voiceless	−	+	−	+	−	+	−	+	−	+	−	+	−	−	+	+	+	+	+	0	0	0	0	0	0	0	0	0	0	0	0	0	0

of German which have been published previously. It is a little difficult to perceive the reasoning leading to the system used by Halle (1954, p. 208), since no thorough explanation of the procedures used for establishing the set of German phonemes is supplied. The same can be said of Meyer-Eppler's modification of the Halle matrix (1959, p. 324).

A more complete distinctive feature analysis of German is given by Heike (1961). This matrix is rather close to ours in terms of its phonemic inventory and the specified features. Heike has not included the infrequently occurring /ž/, but has a /j/ phoneme although, at the same time, he recognizes both syllabic and non-syllabic variants of /i/ and /u/. More will be said of these phonemes later in this section.

In our analysis, the compact *vs.* non-compact and diffuse *vs.* non-diffuse features are utilized, compared with Heike's single feature of compactness. On the other hand, we have chosen the voiced *vs.* voiceless feature for consonants (based on the phonology of the Hochsprache) to specify the differentiation accomplished by Heike's two features, tense *vs.* lax and strident *vs.* mellow. In cases like these, the overall aims of our research have influenced, to some extent, our preference for one of the acceptable analyses. Since the main purpose of this study is the comparison of three phonological systems, we have tended to favor those descriptive solutions which would facilitate this comparison.

Heike's analysis is partially obscured by his separate presentation of features in up to five different positions. Thus, for example, the phoneme /r/ is specified as [−consonantal] after long nuclear phonemes but as [+consonantal] after short nuclear phonemes. Aside from this basic methodological difference, there are a few other disagreements between Heike's analysis and ours, some already mentioned, and some due to such facts as Heike's assignment of the value [+vocalic] to nasals and of the value [+consonantal] to /h/.

Of other phonological descriptions of German, perhaps those which are most widely known are the three of Moulton (1947, 1956, and 1962). It can be seen that our scheme most nearly coincides with Moulton's 1947 phonemic system. In fact, the only difference is that we regard the diphthongs /ai, au, oi/ as consisting of two segmental phonemes each. One point which should be specially mentioned is the fact that we prefer Moulton's early view that [ə] is an allophone of /e/. The examples which Moulton later used to illustrate unstressed [ɛ] in contrast with [ə] consist of very few marginal morphemes, clearly identifiable as loan words and insufficient, in our opinion, to posit a phoneme /ə/ distinct from /e/. To set up /ə/ as a phoneme occurring only in unstressed position in complementary distribution with /e/ which is found, with the exception of a few loans, only in stressed position, seems to us questionable, since it obscures a basic distributional property of German vowels. We realize, of course, that it is not easy to decide which foreign words should be included in the data serving as the basis of the phonological analysis. But unassimilated morphemes of foreign origin clearly must be excluded if the resulting phonemic system is to be realistic. If no such exclusions were made, then a number of phones listed by Siebs, for example the nasal vowels [ã] or [õ] occurring in French words, or the palatal nasal [ɲ] found in Spanish citation words, would have to be included in the phonemic inventory of German.

In our German phonemic system, the affricates [ts], [tš], [dž], and [pf] are interpreted as two-phoneme sequences. This agrees with the analyses of Moulton and Heike and is supported by Morciniec (1958) who bases his conclusion on arguments of parallelism with other elements of the phonemic system and on admissibility criteria in phonological distribution. In German, of course (unlike Czech), there are no minimal pairs distinguished solely by the contrast of an affricate and the corresponding phoneme pair, for example by the contrast [c] *vs.* [ts].

It should also be noted that we interpret the glottal stop as an optional manifestation of disjuncture before vowels (see also Chapter 4), as proposed by Moulton (1947) and accepted by Heike (1961, p. 165). As in most analyses of German, we consider the phones [x] and [ç] to be allophones of the phoneme /x/ (see Moulton, 1947).

The specification of the features for /r/ is admittedly rather difficult. We have reached our conclusion by again basing our scheme consistently on the description of the Hochsprache. Thus, [ʀ] and [r] (the uvular trill and the tongue tip trill, respectively) are in free variation according to regional and personal preferences. The form transcribed as [ʌ] by Viëtor (1921) is discouraged by Siebs.

The phonemes /i/ and /u/ have parallel distributions, occurring either as syllabic nuclei or non-syllabically in prevocalic or postvocalic positions. The prevocalic allophone of /i/ is articulated with a moderate degree of lamino-palatal friction, especially before stressed vowels (see Morciniec, 1958, p. 64). Prevocalic /u/ is rare and occurs in such loans as *Statue* or, with some speakers, in *Januar* and others; in our German corpus, there are only four occurrences of /u/ in this position. The variants of /i/ and /u/ require that the feature vocalic *vs.* non-vocalic for these two phonemes be considered as redundant. As is shown in Chapter 4, the allophones of /i/

and /u/ have a predictable distribution statable without reference to the syllabic nucleus (in contrast to similar phones in Czech and in Russian); the feature syllabic *vs.* non-syllabic is thus unnecessary in the German matrix (see also Moulton, 1947, p. 213).

The Siebs system is, of course, not a phonemic one but rather is based on a relatively broad transcription of German. The Siebs description therefore includes a number of symbols for sounds which in our analysis are considered to have allophonic status and are not designated by separate symbols in the phonemic inventory. It should be especially noted that Siebs' [ɛ:], as in *Käse*, is taken by us to be a spelling pronunciation of *ä* and is not listed as a separate phoneme in our scheme (see also Heike, 1961, pp. 163–165).

3.4. Comparison of Relative Frequencies of Phonemes

Table 4 gives the relative frequencies of all segmental phonemes in Russian, Czech, and German. The frequency figures, expressed in percent, are based on the analysis of the entire set of corpora.

Table 4.—Phoneme frequencies in Russian, Czech, and German

Russian		Czech		German	
Phoneme	*Mean Freq. in pct.*	*Phoneme*	*Mean Freq. in pct.*	*Phoneme*	*Mean Freq. in pct.*
p	2.309	p	3.043	p	1.032
p′	0.475				
b	1.096	b	1.520	b	1.745
b′	0.368				
t	4.266	t	4.878	t	8.869
t′	1.885	ţ	0.991		
d	1.665	d	2.784	d	4.116
d′	1.038	ḑ	0.527		
k	3.175	k	3.559	k	1.919
k′	0.534				
g	1.304	g	0.427	g	1.999
c	0.562	c	1.369		
č	1.633	č	0.991		
f	0.948	f	0.603	f	2.454
f′	0.059				
v	2.978	v	3.627	v	2.086
v′	1.016				
s	3.093	s	4.994	s	4.606
s′	1.863				
z	1.367	z	1.898	z	1.815
z′	0.322				
š	1.564	š	1.345	š	1.731
ž	0.951	ž	0.898	ž	0.005
x	0.987	x	1.040	x	2.664
		h	1.468	h	1.126

(Cont'd.)

Table 4. (*Cont'd.*)

Russian		Czech		German	
Phoneme	Mean Freq. in pct.	Phoneme	Mean Freq. in pct.	Phoneme	Mean Freq. in pct.
m	2.317	m	3.785	m	2.841
m′	0.805				
n	4.100	n	4.492	n	10.068
n′	2.297	ŋ	1.967		
				ŋ	0.683
l	2.664	l	4.981	l	3.500
l′	2.081				
r	2.907	r	2.965	r	7.534
r′	1.381	ř	1.110		
j	4.137	j	3.327		
i	11.351	i	6.425		
		e	9.648	i	6.993
a	12.957	a	6.990	e	11.932
		o	7.785	a	6.336
u	2.134	u	3.166	o	1.704
				u	3.145
				ü	0.351
				ö	0.170
í	2.781	i:	3.562	i:	2.138
é	2.614	e:	1.125	e:	2.566
á	4.629	a:	2.124	a:	1.708
ó	4.026	o:	0.022	o:	0.831
ú	1.361	u:	0.564	u:	0.709
				ü:	0.442
				ö:	0.181

Some interpretations of the comparative frequency figures are attempted in Table 5 which gives a set of comparative phonological indices for the three languages. These indices offer some indications of how the typological and genetic relationships among Russian, Czech, and German are reflected quantitatively. Each index has been computed as the ratio of the relative frequencies of two groups of phonemes identified by conventional articulatory terms. Several of the indices were suggested by W. P. Lehmann (1962, p. 57); others were suggested by the data.

For each index, the absolute value of the difference between the ratios for Czech and Russian is listed as d_s; d_{min} is the absolute value of the difference between the German index and the most nearly equal index value in either of the Slavic languages. The comparison is made more striking by expressing these differences in percentages, i.e. as 100 $d/index_{avg}$. In all but two cases, the Russian and Czech index values are much nearer to each other than either is to that of German, suggesting clearly a correlation between such quantitative phonological indicators and close genetic relationship.

Table 5.—Comparative phonological indices

Index	Russian	Czech	German	d_s	d_{min}	Percent diff.	
						Slavic	German
*vl. cons./vd. cons.	1.666	1.555	1.752	0.111	0.086	6.890	5.032
vl. stop/vd. stop	2.315	2.372	1.504	0.057	0.811	2.375	40.348
stop/fricative	1.196	1.117	1.194	0.079	0.002	6.831	0.167
stop/nasal	1.903	1.731	1.448	0.172	0.283	9.466	17.261
obst./sonorant	1.563	1.589	1.469	0.026	0.094	1.650	6.201
trill/lateral	0.904	0.818	2.153	0.086	1.249	9.988	81.714
**n/other nasal	2.049	1.706	2.857	0.343	0.808	18.269	32.939
total pct. nasal	9.519	10.244	13.592	0.725	3.348	7.337	28.092
total pct. liquid	9.033	9.056	11.034	0.023	1.978	0.254	19.691
total pct. sonorant	22.689	22.627	24.626	0.062	1.937	0.274	8.188

* Including only those phonemes for which the voiced *vs.* voiceless feature is distinctive.

** In Russian, the values for *n* in this index computation included the frequencies of both /n/ and /n'/, and in Czech, of both /n/ and /ŋ/.

Chapter 4

THE PHONOLOGICAL SYLLABLE

It should be emphasized at the outset that the syllabic segment used in our analysis is the phonological, not the phonetic syllable. The reason for this choice was not so much the difficulty inherent in defining and delimiting phonetic syllables, a notoriously elusive problem. Rather, our prime motivation for selecting the phonological syllable was the need for a basic unit of analysis on the phonological level which would make it possible to state in a reasonably revealing manner the tactics of this stratum and which would allow a quantitative study of the combinatory potentialities of phonemes.

It was considered essential that the delimitation of the phonological syllable should satisfy at least the following criteria:

a. The resulting phonological unit should coincide, as much as possible, with the usual notion of the syllable as used in linguistics. Although the phonological syllable is not always defined in descriptive phonological studies which use it and the concept is thus sometimes employed with imprecise and ambiguous meanings, there are, nevertheless, some basic principles in the delimitation of the syllable on which most linguists would agree. As will become apparent later in this chapter, we tried to observe such common-sense criteria in our approach.

b. The general procedure should be applicable to all three languages and should give satisfactory results for each.

c. The segmentation of the phonemic string into syllables should be unambiguous, so that every well-formed string could be divided into a definite number of syllables and precise syllable boundaries could be determined by non-arbitrary procedures.

The basic method for arriving at the phonological syllable is a form of immediate constituent analysis in which the utterance is segmented into a series of hierarchically organized configurations of decreasing complexity. The syllable is the smallest recurrent configuration of phonemes obtainable by this analysis which satisfies certain minimal structural requirements.

Although our method follows in basic outlines and terminology the phonological segmentation of Hockett (as described in his *Manual of Phonology*, 1955), our analysis and our usage of terms differ from Hockett's in several ways. The procedure used in this study was first applied by Kučera to Czech (Kučera, 1961) and later used with some modifications in the analysis of Russian (Kučera, 1963b; Saunders, in preparation). It is presented here only in an outline form with some elucidation of the method as applied to German for which it has not previously been described.

Utterances are analyzed into sequences of *macrosegments* which are defined as strings delimited by a completed intonational contour (either terminal or non-terminal) and bounded by *terminal disjunctures*. Macrosegments can thus coincide with a phonemic phrase or with a simple utterance which is not further subdivided into phonemic phrases. Terminal disjunctures are manifested as pauses of indeterminate length as well as by other distributional phonological characteristics. Common to all three languages is the restriction that voiceless but not voiced obstruents can occur before a terminal disjuncture, either alone or in consonantal clusters. German and Czech have in common the optional occurrence of glottal stop as a manifestation of terminal disjuncture if a syllabic vowel is the next phoneme. German alone shows the aspiration of /p/, /t/, and /k/ immediately following a terminal disjuncture and the allophone [ç] in this position.

Macrosegments can be further analyzed as:

a. Indivisible; no part of the macrosegment has the potentiality to constitute, as the same morphemic unit (i.e. with identical meaning), a macrosegment by itself. In Russian, for example, /dámi/ 'ladies' is an indivisible macrosegment in spite of the fact that /dá/ 'yes' and /mí/ 'we' are possible macrosegments. This is because the criterion of identical meaning is not fulfilled. It should be noted that our procedure refers to the morphemic level in determining the equivalence or lack of equivalence of phonological strings.

b. Divisible into two or more segments, each of which can constitute, as the same morphemic unit, a macrosegment by itself. In German, the macrosegment /me:rmilx/ is a divisible one because two of its segments, namely /me:r/ and /milx/, may each constitute a macrosegment by itself.

c. Divisible into two or more segments some, but not all, of which can constitute, as the same morphemic units, a macrosegment. In Czech, for example, /sprahi/ 'from Prague' is such a macrosegment because /prahi/ may occur as a macrosegment by itself but /s/ may not.

With this information, it is possible to proceed with the minimum definition of the *phonological word*. As will be shown later, this definition will need to be somewhat expanded in each language by considering some other criteria.

A phonological word is any continuous string of segmental phonemes which has the potential of constituting a macrosegment.

The boundaries between phonological words within a macrosegment are marked by the occurrence of *external disjuncture* and denoted by $/+/$. External disjuncture has phonological manifestations similar but not necessarily identical to those of terminal disjuncture. In Russian and in Czech, for example, the opposition voiced *vs.* voiceless is suspended in the phoneme or cluster of phonemes immediately preceding external disjuncture, as it is before terminal disjuncture, but the actual distribution of voiced and voiceless obstruents is different. While only voiceless obstruents may occur before terminal disjunctures, both voiceless and voiced ones may occur before external disjunctures in a predictable distribution determined by the phoneme or phonemes immediately following the external disjuncture. (For a detailed description of this and other manifestations, see Kučera, 1961, pp. 57–61; the situation in Russian is similar as discussed by Saunders, in preparation.)

As already mentioned, the definition of a phonological word needs to be expanded, somewhat differently in each of the three languages, in order to take into account some marginal situations. The problem lies, essentially, in the fact that some isolable segments in each of these languages which cannot, under normal circumstances, constitute macrosegments by themselves, exhibit the phonological properties typical of phonological words, as well as boundary characteristics of external disjuncture rather than those of other disjunctures or of no disjuncture at all.

In Czech, for example, such segments as /se/ 'self' (acc.), /mu/ 'him' (dat.), /ho/ 'him' (acc.) and several others behave like phonological words in terms of their distributional ability to constitute accentual units in the utterance. In Czech, where stress is a configurational feature which alone cannot signal phonemic distinctions but rather organizes the utterance into sequential prosodic units, the accentual units known as the *measure* and the *pre-measure segment* are important determinants of the phonological status of the strings which constitute them. Thus, in Czech, the definition of the phonological word needs to be supplemented by certain considerations of stress and its functions (for details, see Kučera, 1961, pp. 52–61).

Russian resembles the Czech situation, but stress, which in Russian is phonemic (i.e. has the potentiality of differentiating segments with non-identical meanings) cannot alone be used as a simple criterion for determining the status of phonological words. Nevertheless, one finds again in Russian a number of identifiable strings which do not normally constitute macrosegments by themselves but have other characteristics of phonological words. For example, the conjunction *čtob* 'in order to' which is phonemically either /štóp/ or /štób/, depending on the following word, does not normally occur alone but does have other characteristics of a phonological word. One is that it can be stressed even if the stress is frequently of somewhat lesser intensity than that placed on other phonological words. Another is that the manifestation of the final consonantal phoneme as either /p/ or /b/ is the same as we find in phonological words followed by external disjuncture: /b/ occurs only if the next word begins with a voiced obstruent except /v/, or with /v/ plus voiced obstruent;[5] /p/ occurs elsewhere. This is a different situation than that exhibited by morpheme combinations not separated by disjuncture or by morphemes followed by other than the external type of disjuncture. Thus, in order to account properly for this situation, segments like *čtob* must be classed as phonological words. A discussion of the various phonological boundaries in Russian can be found in Halle's *The Sound Pattern of Russian* (1959, pp. 48–50).[6]

Generally speaking, our procedure identified, in both Russian and Czech, those segments which are conventionally classed as "words" from the point of view of grammatical function as being also phonological words; however, prepositions (as well as prefixes) and unstressed enclitics which, as will be shown subsequently, exhibit different phonological characteristics were not considered phonological words.

In German, substitution criteria need to be taken into consideration to isolate as phonological words those segments which behave like other phonological words but do not normally constitute macrosegments by themselves. The following supplementary rule can be formulated:

In addition to those strings which have the potentiality of constituting macrosegments by themselves, all other continuous strings of segmental phonemes which can be isolated from a macrosegment are phonological words (symbolized in the following examples by A) if they can be separated from other segments of the same sequence already known to be phonological words (symbolized by B) by other phonological words (symbolized by C),

---

[5] For a discussion of certain interesting aspects of this Russian phonological phenomenon see Jakobson (1956). A brief evaluation of various descriptions of the distribution of voiced and voiceless obstruents in standard Russian is given by Shapiro (1966).

[6] Since Halle's analytical method is different from ours, he needs to assume additional boundaries in order to formulate various morphophonemic rules. These additional boundaries are not required in our analysis. Neither do we see any need for Halle's special boundary posited to separate the two components of such Russian abbreviation compounds as *gosbank* 'state bank'. Our phonemic transcription in this case does not agree with Halle's rule; we would transcribe the internal cluster of *gosbank* as /zb/, not as /sb/. In this detail, our transcription agrees with the majority of Soviet sources dealing with the phonetics of standard Russian. (For a summary, see Shapiro, 1966.)

but without A being part of C. The following examples of German macro-segments should clarify this procedure (parentheses indicate an element which may or may not be present):

1) (B) B A (B)

in which B's are known to be phonological words, but where A is not yet determined. Given the phonological word C, A is said to be a phonological word if the sequence

2) (B) B C A (B)

is possible. Thus,

3) *Er steht auf* 'He is getting up'

can be considered a specific example of (1). The status of *auf* as a phonological word remains to be determined. Let us take, as C, the word *jetzt* 'now':

4) *Er steht jetzt auf* 'He is getting up now'

is certainly a well-formed sentence. Thus, the so-called separable prefix *auf* is shown to be a phonological word by our criteria. The plausibility of this conclusion is also supported by the fact that *auf* can carry a strong stress of its own, a property of other phonological words in German. The same procedure would identify German prepositions as phonological words.

The inseparable verbal prefixes, on the other hand, can never occur in macrosegments comparable to (3) and thus their status as phonological words cannot be tested by the procedure used above for *auf*. The sentence

5) **Sie fährt es er*

is obviously ungrammatical. This leaves only type (6) to be tested:

6) *Sie wird es erfahren* 'She will learn about it',

in which the status of *erfahren* as one or two phonological words is to be determined. It can be easily seen that the insertion of *bald* 'soon' is admissible in (7) but not in (8):

7) *Sie wird es bald erfahren* 'She will learn about it soon',

8) **Sie wird es er bald fahren*

Consequently, the inseparable prefix *er* is not a phonological word. The fact that inseparable prefixes never have strong stress supports this conclusion.

However, it can also be easily demonstrated that such inseparable prefixes in German as *er*, *be*, etc., although not phonological words, constitute a phonological unit and account for phonological manifestations which logically require an assumption of another kind of boundary or disjuncture between them and the subsequent segment. For example, although *beehren* 'to honor' does not constitute two phonological words, *ehren* 'to honor' is isolable as a phonological word and the boundary between *be* and *ehren* can be signalled by a glottal stop which functions as an optional manifestation of disjuncture before a vowel.

In order to account, in all three languages, for such situations when strings of segmental phonemes manifest specific phonological boundary signals but are themselves *not* phonological words, we assume a third type of disjuncture, *internal disjuncture*, denoted by / = /.

The exact procedures for determining the occurrence of an internal disjuncture in the Slavic languages are quite complex and cannot be described in complete detail here because of space limitations. The reader may find a detailed discussion of this matter in *The Phonology of Czech* (Kučera, 1961, pp. 61–65). In general, internal disjuncture separates, in Russian and in Czech, prepositions and prefixes from the following phonological words. To illustrate this, let us consider an extended version of the Czech example used previously: /je+ s = prahi/ 'He is from Prague' which, as can be seen, includes three segments bounded by disjunctures but only two phonological words, /je/ and /prahi/. The segment /s/ is not a phonological word, since it does not fulfill any of the criteria specified in the definition of phonological words.

The phonological manifestations of internal disjuncture may show some overlap with the manifestations of the two other disjunctures, but are not necessarily identical with them in all cases. For example, the opposition voiced *vs.* voiceless in Russian and in Czech is not suspended before internal disjuncture in all environments, but only if / = / is followed by an obstruent. Compare, for example, the Russian /iz = b'irl'ína/ 'from Berlin', /is = par'íža/ 'from Paris', but /iz = maskví/ 'from Moscow'; in contrast to /s = f'ivral'á/ 'since February', /z = d'ikabr'á/ 'since December' but /s = márta/ 'since March'. These examples illustrate that both /s/ and /z/ are admissible before / = / followed by a sonorant (/m/ in our case) and that their distribution is unpredictable without specification of the actual preposition involved.

Any continuous string of segmental phonemes bounded by any disjuncture on either side is a *microsegment*. Thus, in the cited Czech example /je+ s = prahi/, there is a total of three microsegments (but only two phonological words).

The procedure for the determination of microsegments is not without difficulties; the chief one among them is the fact that it has to rely on potentiality of occurrence as the same morphemic unit (or, to put it differently, on the concept of "identical meaning") which may, under some circumstances, be a matter of subjective judgment. We are fully aware that our method thus requires reference to the morphemic stratum in order to determine the equivalence of two phonological strings for the purposes of specifying the privilege of occurrence of the tested string. While such a procedure may be objected to by conservative structuralists on the grounds that it mixes levels, we consider this method to be consistent with our view of language as a system of systems. At any rate, the procedure has proven to be a workable one, in spite of occasional practical difficulties, and has made it possible to delimit the phonological syllable in a consistent manner, allowing the quantitative analysis of the three languages reported in the subsequent chapters.

4.1. Definition of the Phonological Syllable

The phonological syllable is a constituent of a microsegment. This implies the restriction that phonological syllables may not bridge microsegments, that is, that they may not contain a disjuncture. The problem which this presents in Russian and in Czech, which have microsegments consisting of a single consonantal phoneme, will be discussed in Section 4.3.

Our definition of the phonological syllable consists of specifying its minimum and maximum constituents. The minimum requirement for a phonological syllable is that it contain a *syllabic nucleus* which serves, in all three languages, as the center of stress and of intonational levels. In Russian and in German, only vowels can serve as syllabic nuclei; in Czech, vowels and — under certain circumstances — the phonemes /r/, /l/ and /m/ have this function. The portion of the microsegment following disjuncture and preceding the first syllabic nucleus is the *onset* of the syllable, and the part following the last nucleus up to the next disjuncture is the *coda*. That portion of the microsegment occurring between two successive nuclei is the *interlude*. Our subsequent procedure will divide interludes into sequences of codas and onsets in order to segment the text into a series of distinct syllables. While the nucleus is a prerequisite of a syllable, onsets, codas, and interludes are optional.

Nucleus, onset, coda, and interlude can be subsumed under the joint term of *constituents* of the syllable. The number of sequential phonemes which may compose any such constituent may then be specified and will be subsequently referred to as the number of possible *positions* of a syllabic constituent. The *membership* of each position within a constituent is the set of those segmental phonemes which can occupy the given position.

In Russian, the nucleus consists of a single position and only the vowel

phonemes can occupy it. Any vowel occurrence, i.e. every occurrence of
/i/, /í/, /é/, /a/, /á/, /u/, /ú/, /ó/ in a Russian string, signals the presence of a
syllabic nucleus.

In Czech, the nucleus has one or two positions. A two-position nucleus
consists of the vowel chains /ou/ and /au/ if no disjuncture intervenes
between the vowels. The chain /eu/ is considered to form two successive
syllabic nuclei in our analysis, although some manuals of "standard pronunciation" of Czech accept a monosyllabic /eu/ as a legitimate alternative.

A single position nucleus in Czech is constituted by:

a. any occurrence of a vowel phoneme, i.e. every occurrence of /i/, /i:/,
/e/, /e:/, /a/, /a:/, /u/, /u:/, /o/, /o:/, except when representing a part of a two-
position nucleus;

b. any occurrence of /r/ and /l/ if preceded by a consonant phoneme
and followed by a consonant phoneme or disjuncture; for example, /+prxl+/
'he fled' contains two syllabic nuclei, /r/ and /l/;

c. any occurrence of /m/ if preceded by /d/, /s/ or /z/ and followed by
disjuncture or by /n/ or /d/. For example, /+sedm+/ 'seven' and /+osmna:
ct+/ 'eighteen' contain two syllabic nuclei each.

In German, two-position nuclei consist of the sequences /au/, /ai/ and /oi/
if no disjuncture intervenes between the vowels. All other occurrences of
/i/, /i:/, /ü/, /ü:/, /e/, /e:/, /ö/, /ö:/, /a/, /a:/, /u/, /u:/, /o/, /o:/ constitute
a single position nucleus, except /i/ and /u/ which immediately precede
another vowel without a disjuncture intervening. Such prevocalic /i/ or /u/,
which are realized by the allophones [j] and [w] respectively, are considered in our analysis to be members of onsets.

Onsets in Russian have from zero to four positions, occupied by the
consonant phonemes and the semivowel /j/. The same is true of Czech. In
German, onsets have from zero to three positions, filled by consonants and
the non-syllabic vowels. The following examples illustrate the onset types
found in our data. O is a general symbol for the phonemes that can occupy
the respective positions. The disjunctures delimiting the segments are included
in the examples to emphasize the microsegment status of the strings.

Russian	*Onset type*
/+ón+/ 'he'	zero
/+sín+/ 'son'	O
/+f's'ó+/ 'everything'	OO
/+strás't'+/ 'passion'	OOO
/+fstr'éča+/ 'encounter'	OOOO

Czech

		Onset type
/ + on + /	'he'	zero
/ + sin + /	'son'	O
/ + fše + /	'everything'	OO
/ + strast + /	'distress'	OOO
/ + pštros + /	'ostrich'	OOOO

German

		Onset type
/ + ain + /	'one', 'a'	zero
/ + bet + /	'bed'	O
/ + glat + /	'smooth'	OO
/ + pflixt + /	'duty'	OOO

Codas in Russian have from zero to four positions and can be filled by consonants or the semivowel /j/. In Czech, codas have from zero to three positions, occupied by consonants or the semivowel /j/. In German, codas, as evidenced in our data analyzed for this study, have from zero to four positions, although instances of a five position coda have been suggested (Moulton, 1956, p. 376; Menzerath, 1954, p. 68). The phonemes representing the membership of coda positions are symbolized by C in the following examples. Since the examples are intended to reflect the syllabic structures found in our corpora, no five-position codas are listed for German.

Russian

		Coda type
/ + já + /	'I'	zero
/ + stój + /	'stop!'	C
/ + kós't' + /	'bone'	CC
/ + tólst + /	'fat'	CCC
/ + čórstf + /	'stale'	CCCC

Czech

		Coda type
/ + ja: + /	'I'	zero
/ + stu:j + /	'stop!'	C
/ + kost + /	'bone'	CC
/ + za:pst + /	'to freeze'	CCC

German

		Coda type
/+da:+/	'there', 'since'	zero
/+bax+/	'brook'	C
/+glaupt+/	'(he) believes'	CC
/+folkt+/	'(he) follows'	CCC
/+herpst+/	'autumn'	CCCC

The membership of each position of an onset or a coda (i.e. the set of segmental phonemes which may occupy such position) varies greatly depending on the type of onset or coda or, in other words, on the total number of positions filled in the particular syllable. So, for example, the onset position immediately preceding the nucleus in Czech can be occupied by all the consonant phonemes and the semivowel /j/ in a one-position onset; however, in a four-position onset only /n ŋ r ř v j l/ can occur immediately preceding the nucleus. This type of restriction on membership, which depends on the number of positions filled, is an important consideration in the further analysis of the syllable. For this reason, the generalized scheme of the syllable for the three languages presented below includes, by means of subscripts, an indication of the position in relation to the nucleus as well as the type of the constituents in terms of the number of positions filled. The letter N designates a nucleus position, the letter O an onset position, and the letter C a coda position. The first subscript digit, in both the onset and coda symbols, indicates the type of the constituent; the second subscript digit represents the numbering of the positions, always counting away from the nucleus. Thus, for example, the symbol O_{31} indicates the first position of a three-member onset to the left of the nucleus.

The following is a generalized scheme of the syllable (disregarding, for the present, the problem of interludes) for the three languages analyzed here. It should be remembered that certain of the positions specified in the scheme apply only to one or two of the languages. A four-position onset is not applicable in German, a four-position coda is not applicable in Czech, and a two-position nucleus is not applicable in Russian.

$$\begin{bmatrix} & & & O_{11} \\ & & O_{22} & O_{21} \\ & O_{33} & O_{32} & O_{31} \\ O_{44} & O_{43} & O_{42} & O_{41} \end{bmatrix} \quad \begin{matrix} N \\ N_1 \ N_2 \end{matrix} \quad \begin{bmatrix} C_{11} & & & \\ C_{21} & C_{22} & & \\ C_{31} & C_{32} & C_{33} & \\ C_{41} & C_{42} & C_{43} & C_{44} \end{bmatrix}$$

The above scheme should not be taken to imply that syllables of the maximum theoretical length are actually attested in our data or even necessarily in the language. The scheme is simply a way to represent conveniently the structure of the syllable as it is utilized in subsequent analysis.

Examples of monosyllabic phonological words exhibiting any of the possible combinations of onsets and codas up to two positions in length for each constituent are easy to find in all three languages. When it comes to three- and four-position onsets and codas, definite combinatory restrictions, either absolute or probabilistic, become apparent.

In the Slavic languages, there is a strong tendency to avoid an imbalance in the structure of the syllable which would result from combining maximum and minimum length constituents. Combinations of zero onsets with maximum length codas and, conversely, four-position onsets with zero codas occur only in microsegments of marginal status. No monosyllabic phonological words consisting of a four-position onset and a zero coda are attested in our data for either Russian or Czech although, in Czech, one can find some marginal microsegments of this composition, e.g. the archaisms /+lstni:+/ 'cunning', /+mstni:+/ 'revengeful'. But phonological words with three-position onset and zero coda can be found in our data (e.g. Czech /+sklo+/ 'glass', Russian /+mgla+/ 'fog') although they are not very frequent, especially in the Russian corpus. Similarly, zero onsets and three- and four-position codas occur within the syllable in the Slavic languages only marginally, in loan words and foreign citation words.

In German, on the other hand, there is much less resistance to combining maximum and minimum length syllable constituents within the same microsegment. Examples of monosyllabic phonological words consisting of three-position onsets and zero codas can be cited (e.g. /+štro:+/ 'straw'); similarly zero onsets combine with four-position codas, as in /+ernst+/ 'serious', /+artst+/ 'physician', etc. And in some special situations (not attested in our data), such as the genitive suffix −s after four-consonant clusters, we can even find a zero onset and a five-position coda within one syllable, as in /+ernsts+/ 'Ernest's'.

At the opposite end of the scale, combinations of maximum length constituents, i.e. the longest possible onset and coda within a single syllable, are most severely restricted in Czech where there are no four-position onset and three-position coda syllables, or even three-position onset and three-position coda ones. In Russian, there are no syllables of potentially maximum length, i.e. consisting of a four-position onset plus a four-position coda. Monosyllabic combinations of a three-position onset and a four-position coda may be found in such segments as the inflected form of a prefixed word, $/+ \text{pra} = \text{stranstf}+/$ 'spaces' (gen.), but they do not occur at all in our Russian corpus.

In German, three-position onsets plus four-position codas are attested, for example, $/+ \text{ge} = \text{pflantst}+/$ 'seeded'.

Certain syllabic structures, although admissible, have very low frequencies of occurrence. The most revealing examples of this kind can be cited from the analysis of monosyllabic microsegments in which there are no interludes to be divided and thus no possibility of interpretative interference with the language structure. Our Russian and Czech data, for which we have a complete analysis of microsegment composition available, illustrate well the interrelationship between syllabic structure and occurrence frequency.

There are altogether 8,380 monosyllabic microsegments in our Russian corpus, 10,280 monosyllabic microsegments in our Czech data. Not too surprisingly, the frequency of occurrence of such microsegments is in inverse relationship to their length. In Russian, for example, microsegments consisting of one-position onset + nucleus + zero coda ($= O_1 + N + C_0$, i.e. consisting of two phonemes) are twice as frequent as those whose composition is $O_1 + N + C_1$, i.e. three phonemes. In Czech, the differential in the occurrence frequency of these two syllabic types is is even greater. But occurrence frequency is affected not only by the length of the segment but also by its syllabic structure. In both Russian and Czech, monosyllabic microsegments two phonemes in length and with the structure $O_0 + N + C_1$ are much less frequent than the longer, three phoneme microsegments of the structure $O_1 + N + C_1$. This example reflects, of course, the characteristic sparsity of zero onsets in the Slavic languages. But our data also show that four-phoneme microsegments of the structure $O_1 + N + C_2$ are significantly rarer than microsegments of the same length but of the structure $O_2 + N + C_1$. This example, as well as some other data in the following table, reflect the preference of the Slavic languages for initial clusters as opposed to final clusters.

Table 6 lists, for Russian and Czech, the actual occurrence frequencies of monosyllabic microsegments of different structure as well as their relative frequencies in percentages. For Czech, which has simple and compound syllabic nuclei, the symbol N in the table designates both.

Most of the frequency figures for Russian and Czech are comparable but there are a few interesting differences, the chief among them being the much higher frequency in Czech of monosyllabic microsegments with a three-position onset. This and related differences are traceable, at least in

Table 6.—Frequency distribution of monosyllabic microsegments by syllabic structure

Syllabic structure	Russian		Czech	
	Frequency	%	Frequency	%
$O_0 + N + C_0$	1378	16.444	1319	12.831
$O_0 + N + C_1$	663	7.912	303	2.947
$O_0 + N + C_2$	0	0.000	2	0.019
$O_0 + N + C_3$	0	0.000	0	0.000
$O_0 + N + C_4$	1	0.012	0	0.000
$O_1 + N + C_0$	3143	37.506	4660	45.331
$O_1 + N + C_1$	1621	19.344	1836	17.860
$O_1 + N + C_2$	118	1.408	123	1.196
$O_1 + N + C_3$	7	0.084	1	0.010
$O_1 + N + C_4$	0	0.000	0	0.000
$O_2 + N + C_0$	982	11.718	973	9.465
$O_2 + N + C_1$	414	4.940	918	8.930
$O_2 + N + C_2$	17	0.203	16	0.156
$O_2 + N + C_3$	1	0.012	0	0.000
$O_2 + N + C_4$	0	0.000	0	0.000
$O_3 + N + C_0$	6	0.071	91	0.885
$O_3 + N + C_1$	28	0.334	29	0.282
$O_3 + N + C_2$	1	0.012	9	0.088
$O_3 + N + C_3$	0	0.000	0	0.000
$O_3 + N + C_4$	0	0.000	0	0.000
$O_4 + N + C_0$	0	0.000	0	0.000
$O_4 + N + C_1$	0	0.000	0	0.000
$O_4 + N + C_2$	0	0.000	0	0.000
$O_4 + N + C_3$	0	0.000	0	0.000
$O_4 + N + C_4$	0	0.000	0	0.000
Total	8380	100.000	10280	100.000

part, to somewhat divergent historical changes in these closely related languages.

4.2. Retrieval of Syllables and Division of Interludes

The mechanical retrieval of all distinct onsets and codas from the phonemically transcribed corpora presented little difficulty because our phonemic transcriptions included, in each case, precise indications of the location of disjunctures. It was thus only necessary to scan the phonemic string from each disjuncture up to the immediately following nucleus to isolate an onset. Similarly, scanning of the string to the left of each disjuncture up to the immediately preceding nucleus retrieved the codas. The scanning of the transcribed texts and the retrieval of onsets and codas was accomplished with the aid of computer programs written for the IBM 7070 system. The programs compiled tables of all distinct onsets and tables containing all distinct codas found in each corpus; the frequency of occurrence of each onset and coda was entered in the tables.

At this stage of the processing, we thus had available to us a dictionary of onsets and codas, as represented in each of our corpora. This still left us the problem of analyzing the interludes. Since our approach required the determination of a definite set of syllables and of their frequencies in each corpus, it was necessary to identify syllabic boundaries in each case, including those in microsegments which had more than one nucleus and thus contained syllabic interludes.

The problem of interlude assignment to the surrounding syllables has been a frequent topic of discussion in linguistic literature.[7] In our method, interludes are considered to consist of a portion (which may be zero) assignable as a coda to the left-hand syllable, followed by a portion (which also may be zero) assignable as an onset to the right-hand syllable.

The governing principle of our procedure for interlude division has been to base the segmentation on the phonological structuring of the onsets and the codas already observed in our data. Operationally, this principle was implemented by two ordered rules:

1) Whenever possible, the interlude should be divided in such a manner that the coda and onset obtained would not enlarge the set of distinct codas and onsets already established.

2) If the first rule does not provide a division or if, on the other hand, it allows more than one acceptable interlude division, then that division is preferred which is statistically favored because of the frequency distribution of onsets and codas of the various types occurring immediately after or immediately before disjuncture respectively.

A detailed explanation and illustration of the statistical factors operating in the second rule are given below.[8]

Since the two rules are ordered, the computer program which divided

---

[7] Criteria for phonological syllabification have been suggested by Kuryłowicz (1948), O'Connor and Trim (1953), Haugen (1956), and others.

[8] Twaddell (1936) has made a study of interlude types for German and has suggested several criteria for their division. His basic criterion is equivalent to our first rule, but the others make use of various phonological information in the adjacent syllabic nuclei. Although our principles for interlude division are similar to criteria proposed by other linguists, they are not identical with any of them. Our second rule of interlude division, as will become apparent in subsequent discussion, is based on the consideration of the statistical information retrieved from the corpus and utilized as an indicator of the phonological structure of the language. It should be particularly noted that the interlude division method used in the present study is not the same as the procedure described by Kučera in *The Phonology of Czech* (1961, pp. 81–83), but represents a further development of the 1961 approach.

interludes considered initially only the first rule. If the first rule offered an acceptable *and* a unique interlude division, the second rule was not taken into consideration. The following examples from each language will illustrate this simple situation.

The Russian microsegment /l′éxči/ 'easier' contains two nuclei and the interlude /xč/. The interlude could be assigned to the first or to the second nucleus in three different ways (potential interlude division is indicated by a dot):

  i)   /l′é.xči/
  ii) /l′éx.či/
  iii) /l′éxč.i/

Division i) is rejected because it would enlarge the established set of onsets; there are no /xč/ onsets in Russian. Division iii) is rejected because it would expand the set of codas; no /xč/ codas are attested. However, division ii) is acceptable because it does not enlarge either the set of codas or onsets (/x/ codas and /č/ onsets are common in Russian). Since this division is also the only one possible, the microsegment will be divided into two syllables as indicated in ii) and the second interlude division rule will not need to be considered.

The Czech microsegment /mušstvo/ 'team' contains two syllabic nuclei /u/ and /o/. The interlude between them, /šstv/, can be divided into coda and onset in five different ways:

  i)   /mušstv.o/
  ii) /mušst.vo/
  iii) /mušs.tvo/
  iv) /muš.stvo/
  v)   /mu.šstvo/

Division i) can be eliminated without further consideration because it would necessitate the introduction of four-position codas which otherwise do not exist in Czech. Divisions ii) and iii) would enlarge the set of codas (no /šst/ or /šs/ codas exist in Czech); division v) would enlarge the set of onsets (no /šstv/ onset is attested). This leaves, as the only solution, division iv) which is acceptable because it does not result in any expansion of the set of onsets and codas. Again, there is no need to proceed to the second interlude division rule.

Finally, let us consider the German example /merkba:r/ 'noticeable' which contains two syllabic nuclei, /e/ and /a:/. The interlude /rkb/ has four possibilities of division:

    i) /me.rkba:r/
    ii) /mer.kba:r/
    iii) /merk.ba:r/
    iv) /merkb.a:r/

Divisions i) and ii) would enlarge the set of onsets and division iv) the set of codas. These three divisions are therefore rejected. The only acceptable division is provided by iii) and the second rule need not be considered.

The problem is more complicated if the first rule does not provide a division (which is in our experience rare) or if it allows more than one acceptable division (which happens fairly frequently). In such cases, the computer program performing the syllabification applied the second rule, according to procedures described in detail below.

It will be recalled that the initial scanning of our phonemically transcribed data provided us with a "dictionary" of onsets and codas, as well as with figures giving the frequency of occurrence of each distinct onset and coda in the respective corpus. Table 7 lists these relative occurrence frequencies in percent, before interludes had been divided. The relative frequencies are given for both onsets and codas by constituent type (*type* referring here to the number of phonemes composing the syllabic constituent).

Table 7.—Frequency of onset and coda types before interlude division

Type	Frequency of occurrence in percent		
	Russian	*Czech*	*German*
O_0	16.865	11.683	23.998
O_1	63.259	62.712	62.838
O_2	18.989	23.624	12.071
O_3	0.830	1.968	1.093
O_4	0.057	0.013	—
C_0	63.230	73.216	21.475
C_1	35.677	25.574	61.548
C_2	1.035	1.206	15.296
C_3	0.048	0.004	1.528
C_4	0.010	—	0.153

Table 7 shows clearly, first of all, that the frequency of non-zero onsets and codas decreases rapidly as their length (in number of phonemes) increases. This suggested our principal statistical indicator for interlude division under rule (2): that division is to be preferred which results in minimum length constituents, i.e. in a coda and an onset each of which has the least possible number of positions. In other words, the difference between the number of phonemes of the resulting coda and the number of phonemes of the resulting onset should be as small as possible.

If we take, for example, an interlude of four phonemes, i.e. the string AZZZZA (where A = any nuclear phoneme, Z = any non-nuclear phoneme), then the first division preference will be AZZ.ZZA (where the dot indicates the interlude division), simply because this will produce the shortest possible coda and onset. Such a division was thus preferred in the execution of our syllabification program if it was admissible (in addition to some other division) under rule (1) or, alternatively, if rule (1) had provided no division.

In certain cases, of course, the principle that the interlude division should result in the shortest possible coda and onset is not an unambiguous criterion. This is true, for example, if the interlude consists of an odd number of phonemes or if the optimal division is inadmissible under rule (1). In such cases, a scale of preferences must be established for the other possible divisions. In our procedure, this scale is based again on the statistical information in Table 7. If alternate interlude divisions are possible, then the longer of the two constituents produced by each such division is compared with the frequency data and the statistically supported division is preferred.

Let us consider, for example, the string AZZZA. The division AZ.ZZA will create a two-phoneme onset (as well as a one-phoneme coda, of course), while the division AZZ.ZA will create a two-phoneme coda. Table 7 shows that two-phoneme onsets occur about twenty times more frequently than two-phoneme codas in Russian and in Czech; on the other hand, two-phoneme codas occur more frequently than two-phoneme onsets in German. Thus the string AZZZA is divided as AZ.ZZA in Russian and in Czech, but as AZZ.ZA in German.

The basic underlying principle of our interlude division consists thus in utilizing the clues of the language structure itself to resolve ambiguous situations.

Table 8 shows the scale of preference of various interlude divisions. It should be emphasized that many low-preference divisions were never utilized in our syllabification. The reader should also note that the number of alternative divisions for long interludes is severely limited by the requirement of division rule (1) that no inadmissible types of onsets and codas (e.g. a four-phoneme coda in Czech) should be produced by the interlude division.

Table 8.—Scale of preference for interlude divisions

Interlude type	Russian	Czech	German	Preference
AZA	A.ZA	A.ZA	A.ZA	1st
	AZ.A	AZ.A	AZ.A	2nd
AZZA	AZ.ZA	AZ.ZA	AZ.ZA	1st
	A.ZZA	A.ZZA	AZZ.A	2nd
	AZZ.A	AZZ.A	A.ZZA	3rd
AZZZA	AZ.ZZA	AZ.ZZA	AZZ.ZA	1st
	AZZ.ZA	AZZ.ZA	AZ.ZZA	2nd
	A.ZZZA	A.ZZZA	AZZZ.A	3rd
	AZZZ.A	AZZZ.A	A.ZZZA	4th
AZZZZA	AZZ.ZZA	AZZ.ZZA	AZZ.ZZA	1st
	AZ.ZZZA	AZ.ZZZA	AZZZ.ZA	2nd
	AZZZ.ZA	AZZZ.ZA	AZ.ZZZA	3rd
	A.ZZZZA	A.ZZZZA	AZZZZ.A	4th
	AZZZZ.A	—	—	5th
AZZZZZA	AZZ.ZZZA	AZZ.ZZZA	AZZZ.ZZA	1st
	AZZZ.ZZA	AZZZ.ZZA	AZZ.ZZZA	2nd
	AZ.ZZZZA	AZ.ZZZZA	AZZZZ.ZA	3rd
	AZZZZ.ZA	—	—	4th
AZZZZZZA	AZZZ.ZZZA	AZZZ.ZZZA	AZZZ.ZZZA	1st
	AZZ.ZZZZA	AZZ.ZZZZA	AZZZZ.ZZA	2nd
	AZZZZ.ZZA	—	—	3rd
AZZZZZZZA	AZZZ.ZZZZA	AZZZ.ZZZZA	AZZZZ.ZZZA	1st
	AZZZZ.ZZZA	—	—	2nd

4.3. Isolated Consonantal Microsegments in Russian and in Czech

Several Russian and Czech examples cited previously in this chapter
show that the principles for determining disjuncture occurrence isolate
some microsegments consisting of a single consonant; actually, in some
cases, consonantal microsegments can also be composed of a two-consonant
cluster. All of these microsegments are bounded on the right by internal
disjuncture / = / and serve as prepositions and prefixes. Such strings as
these, most of them phonologically identical in Russian and in Czech, (for
example, /+ v = / 'in', /+ s = / 'with, from', /+ k = / 'to', /+ vz = / 'up',
prefix, also with some other meanings) are referred to in further discussion as *isolated consonantal microsegments*. These microsegments, very
few in number (as Table 15 shows), form accentual units with the successive phonological word. They do not contain a syllabic nucleus and do
not constitute syllables by our criteria. Because of our restriction that

a syllable may not extend across a disjuncture, these microsegments cannot be considered as part of the preceding or of the following syllable. They are therefore special *pre-syllabic segments.*[9]

In the informational analysis reported in this monograph, isolated consonantal microsegments in Russian and in Czech have been included in the various calculations on a level equivalent to syllables. German has no isolated consonantal microsegments.

4.4. Phoneme Membership of Syllabic Positions

The division of interludes does not affect the general scheme of syllable structure presented on p. 44. The first rule for interlude division assures that no new positions are added to the onsets or codas represented in the corpus before the division.

The phonemes which occupy a specific position in the syllable structure are said to constitute the *membership* of the position. As was pointed out previously, the membership of a position varies greatly, depending on the type of onset, coda, or nucleus (i.e. on the positions actually filled) which is being described. It is therefore necessary, for example, to specify the membership of an onset position immediately preceding the nucleus separately for one-position onsets, two-position onsets, etc., since these membership sets will differ considerably.

Tables 9, 10, and 11 list the memberships for all syllabic positions in the three languages. The lists are not intended to account for all admissible syllables but rather to describe our data only. They specify the membership of the various positions after interludes have been divided. A plus sign ($+$) should be read as 'and', and a minus sign ($-$) as 'except'.

In considering the membership lists of Russian and of Czech, it should be remembered that /j/ is classed in both languages as a semivowel, so that statements specifying "all consonants" do *not* pertain to /j/. Two-position isolated consonantal microsegments are designated as I_{22} I_{21}, where the second subscript digit represents the position (counting away from the internal disjuncture which delimits the microsegment on the right). For example, in /+ vz = /, /v/ occupies position I_{22}, and /z/ position I_{21}.

---

[9] The problem of isolated consonantal microsegments in Russian is discussed by Saunders (1966) who has proposed several alternative solutions. The approach adopted in this book still strikes us as having the best linguistic justification and as being the most practical one of those solutions mentioned by Saunders. It is the only one of the available alternatives which takes all the important phonological facts (i.e. the manifestations of internal disjuncture) into account and which, at the same time, makes it possible to identify a manageable set of different syllabic structures of a language and allows a rigorous study of the phonotactics as reflected in the composition of the phonological syllable.

Table 9.—Syllabic position memberships in Russian

Nucleus positions:
N = all vowels

Onset positions:
O_{11} = all consonants + /j/
O_{21} = all consonants − /b′ f š x/ + /j/
O_{22} = all consonants − /k′ f′ v′ m′ r′/ + /j/
O_{31} = /t t′ č v n l l′ r r′/
O_{32} = /p t d k g s s′ š/
O_{33} = /t č f v s z š ž m l′/
O_{41} = /l′ r′/
O_{42} = /t g/
O_{43} = /s z/
O_{44} = /f v/

Coda positions:
C_{11} = all consonants − /k′/ + /j/
C_{21} = all consonants − /p′ b′ d d′ k′ c č f′ v′ m′ r′/ + /j/
C_{22} = /p t t′ d d′ k g č s s′ x m n n′ l l′ r r′/
C_{31} = /s n r j/
C_{32} = /t d k g s′/
C_{33} = /t′ f s z l r/
C_{41} = /m r/
C_{42} = /s/
C_{43} = /t/
C_{44} = /f/

Isolated consonantal microsegment positions:
I_{11} = /k g f f′ v v′ s s′ z z′ š ž/
I_{21} = /s z z′/
I_{22} = /f v/

The membership specifications, as given in Tables 9, 10, and 11, simply state the fact of occurrence and, by implication, of non-occurrence of certain phonemes in the various syllabic positions of our corpora. In practice, this may mean that a phoneme which occurred only once in a given position is listed side by side with a phoneme which has a frequency of several hundred occurrences. In order to summarize these quantitative differences in phoneme memberships, Tables 12, 13, and 14 have been included. These tables show the frequency of occurrence of each phoneme in each position; the figure found at the intersection of a phoneme column and of a position row represents the total frequency of the respective phoneme in that position in our entire corpus for that language, after interludes have been divided.

An inspection of Tables 12, 13, and 14 will reveal a number of quantitative divergencies among the three languages which point to significant differences

Table 10.—Syllabic position memberships in Czech

Nucleus positions:

N = all vowels + /l r m/ (with restrictions defined above)
N_1 = /o a/
N_2 = /u/

Onset positions:

O_{11} = all consonants + /j/
O_{21} = all consonants − /g f/ + /j/
O_{22} = all consonants − /ţ ḑ n ņ/ + /j/
O_{31} = /b t d ţ ḑ k v m n ņ l r ř j/
O_{32} = /p t d k v s z ž m ř/
O_{33} = /t d k č f v s z š x h m j/
O_{41} = /ř j/
O_{42} = /t v/
O_{43} = /k s/
O_{44} = /t f s/

Coda positions

C_{11} = all consonants + /j/
C_{21} = all consonants − /b d ţ ḑ g v ņ/
C_{22} = /t d ţ ḑ k g c č f s š ž m ř/
C_{31} = /m/
C_{32} = /š/
C_{33} = /t/

Isolated consonantal microsegment positions:

I_{11} = /k g f v s z/
I_{21} = /s z/
I_{22} = /f v/

Table 11.—Syllabic position memberships in German

Nucleus positions:

N = all vowels
N_1 = /a o/
N_2 = /i u/

Onset positions:

O_{11} = all consonants + /i u/
O_{21} = all consonants − /b d g z x h ŋ/ + /i/
O_{22} = /p b t d k g f s š/
O_{31} = /v s l r/
O_{32} = /p t k f s/
O_{33} = /p t s š/

Coda positions:

C_{11} = all consonants − /ž h/
C_{21} = all consonants − /b d g v z ž h/
C_{22} = all consonants − /b g z ž h ŋ/
C_{31} = /p t k f x m n ŋ l r/
C_{32} = /p t k f s š x m n/
C_{33} = /t f s/
C_{41} = /n l r/
C_{42} = /p t n/
C_{43} = /s/
C_{44} = /t/

in their organization of the phonological syllable. The frequency figures will also be utilized in our calculation of the Isotopy Index in Chapter 6.

Since Tables 12, 13, and 14 are organized in such a way as to group together the phoneme frequencies of those positions which belong to the same type of onset or coda, they also contain the information about the relative frequency of onsets and codas with a specific number of positions. For example, the sum of frequencies in the O_{21} and O_{22} rows represents the total frequency of all phonemes occurring in two-position onsets or, in other words, exactly twice the number of two-position onsets in the corpus.

In considering the Czech frequency figures given in Table 13, the reader should keep in mind that in Czech the consonantal phonemes /r/, /l/, and /m/ may function, under specific circumstances defined earlier in this chapter, as syllabic nuclei. The sum of the frequencies of these phonemes in the various onset and coda positions in Table 13 does therefore not represent their total number of occurrences in the Czech corpus. In order to obtain such a total for these three phonemes, their frequencies as syllabic nuclei have to be added to their frequencies in onsets and codas. In our corpus, /r/ occurred as a syllabic nucleus 266 times, /l/ 259 times, and /m/ 6 times.

Table 12.

Frequencies of Russian phonemes in individual positions of onsets, codas, and isolated consonantal microsegments

	p	p'	b	b'	t	t'	d	d'	k	k'	g	c	č	f	f'	v	v'	s	s'	z	z'	š	ž	x	m	m'	n	n'	l	l'	r	r'	j	Total by type
O_{11}	1357	428	790	362	1774	1147	1109	763	1805	455	782	475	1259	66	29	1915	788	659	656	797	91	579	754	402	1174	751	2923	1920	1179	1314	1318	766	2740	33327
O_{21}	14	27	2	2	609	48	36	70	308	79	3	1	89		3	399	172	3	190	1	12	1	5		60	44	214	131	386	268	770	518	27	8978
O_{22}	727	16	110	4	293	80	168	61	315		256	4	18	210		106		985	205	192	28	442	26	70	100		10	3	3	5	14		38	
O_{31}	7					1	24		21		7		1			10			1	9			2				2					9	9	525
O_{32}					113								1					1				1							9	4	138			
O_{33}					2									2		15		136				2			5					1				
O_{41}					11						1																							48
O_{42}														11		1																		
O_{43}																		11																
O_{44}																																	11	
C_{11}	199	4	191		1397	502	322	133	614		234	82	247	377	26	223	19	929	611	283	135	518	153	504	959	10	909	213	1075	462	624	72	1308	13337
C_{21}	2		3		9	7	5	11	3		2			1		1		35	96	19	25	16	3	4	6		37	7	5	22	37	5	23	726
C_{22}	3				50	99			20		1		18					59	37					7	12		2	23	6	4	1			
C_{31}					5	1	1		2					4				4	1								3				2	2		30
C_{32}																		1	1												2	2		
C_{33}																													1					
C_{41}																									1									8
C_{42}														2																				
C_{43}																		2																
C_{44}																														1	1			
I_{11}									87		17			265	1	278	37	258	66	37	28	6	8											1088
I_{21}														10		30		10		27	3													80
I_{22}																																		
Total	2309	475	1096	368	4266	1885	1665	1038	3175	534	1304	562	1633	948	59	2978	1016	3093	1863	1367	322	1564	951	987	2317	805	4100	2297	2664	2081	2907	1381	4137	58147

Table 13.

Frequencies of Czech phonemes in individual positions of onsets, codas, and isolated consonantal microsegments

	p	b	t	d	ť	ď	k	g	c	č	f	v	s	z	š	ž	x	h	m	n	ŋ	l	r	ř	j	Total by type
O₁₁	1605	1188	2521	1567	795	486	2039	55	941	695	113	2128	1474	1061	430	697	294	939	1776	3419	1642	2585	1136	400	2247	32232
O₂₁ / O₂₂	127 / 1098	24 / 101	505 / 383	301 / 253	121	25	232 / 424	244	22 / 6	6 / 47	150	377 / 365	327 / 1157	27 / 262	126 / 157	8 / 7	5 / 115	12 / 299	109 / 342	315	268	946 / 20	1071 / 11	626 / 8	237 / 368	11634
O₃₁ / O₃₂ / O₃₃	33			39 / 9 / 7	2	5	4 / 18 / 6			3	3	7 / 120 / 47	73 / 241	14 / 32	7	33	6	16	33 / 17 / 4	2	18	36	122	25 / 2	112 / 69	1335
O₄₁ / O₄₂ / O₄₃ / O₄₄			1				2					2	1 / 1											1	2	12
C₁₁	179	206	1095	590	64	10	700	105	388	237	124	346	1246	235	558	142	610	197	1481	695	39	1130	352	43	283	11055
C₂₁ / C₂₂			9 / 193		9	1	16 / 11	2	10 / 2	1 / 2	2 / 2		171 / 44	20	9 / 57	1 / 10	10	5	13 / 3	61		6	7	4 / 1	9	710
C₃₁ / C₃₂ / C₃₃			1												1				1							3
I₁₁							107	21			190	202	241	214												975
I₂₁ / I₂₂											18	33		33												102
Total	3043	1520	4878	2784	991	527	3559	427	1369	991	603	3627	4994	1898	1345	898	1040	1468	3779	4492	1967	4722	2699	1110	3327	58058

Table 14.—Frequencies of German phonemes in individual positions of onsets and codas

	p	b	t	d	k	g	f	v	s	z	š	ž	x	h	m	n	ŋ	l	r	i	u	Total by type
O₁₁	280	1558	2741	4179	974	1803	1598	1949	373	1908	614	4	431	1184	1814	2189	198	1648	1128	386	4	26963
O₂₁	104	269	455	110	2	294	63	132	870		17	1			49	88		591	921	2		6590
O₂₂	151		1102		215		221		11		922											
O₃₁	87		79		1		15	97	3									16	163			837
O₃₂	15		97		.				97		162											
O₃₃									5													
C₁₁	285	7	1068	20	495	5	442	15	1902	1	73		1767		1040	6289	402	876	4827			19514
C₂₁	95		304	20	142		95	1	343		3		474		43	1663	84	470	772			8976
C₂₂	33		2971		136		121		852		29		78		27	218		1	1			
C₃₁	6		47		12		1		139		2		48		12	114	34	59	95			1284
C₃₂	8		190		41		19		207				4		3	22						
C₃₃			215				6															
C₄₁	21		18						41							4		20	17			164
C₄₂			41													2						
C₄₃																						
C₄₄																						
Total	1085	1834	9328	4329	2018	2102	2581	2194	4843	1909	1822	5	2802	1184	2988	10589	718	3681	7924	388	4	64328

Chapter 5

COMMUNICATIONAL ANALYSIS
OF THE SYLLABLE

The first part of this chapter gives the basic statistical data on the syllable composition of the three corpora: the number of syllables of various types, the ratios of running syllables to distinct syllables, and detailed information about syllable length in phonemes. The second part of the chapter outlines the procedures and reports the results of several entropy computations for Russian, Czech, and German in which the phonological syllable served as the basic unit of calculation.

5.1. Number of Syllables in the Three Corpora

Table 15 gives a summary of the total number of syllables after the complete syllabification of each corpus. Information about the number and the relative frequency of syllables by length (in terms of constituent phonemes) is included.

Table 15 shows, among other things, that the number of distinct syllables in the corpus is proportional to the number of segmental phonemes of the respective language. In Russian, the ratio of segmental phonemes to distinct syllables is 1 to 73.9, in Czech 1 to 75.3 and in German, 1 to 76.2. The Russian and the Czech corpora were exactly the same in length (100,000 phonemes each), the German corpus approximately 5% longer than the other two (105,174 phonemes). This difference may account for the slightly higher ratio of phonemes to distinct syllables in German. The phoneme/distinct-syllable ratios in three languages, whose syllabic structure and informational use of syllables differ considerably, are rather surprisingly close. This suggests that it might be also of interest to investigate the rate of increase of the set of distinct syllables as a function of the size of the sample, and to try to determine whether some universal linguistic properties — similar to those exhibited by the rate of change in the type/token ratios in the study of vocabulary in different sized samples — are manifested also on the syllable level.

Table 15 offers some information as well on the degree of coding efficiency, as far as syllables are concerned, with interesting variations observable between the Slavic languages and German.

If the aim in constructing a communication system were simply efficiency

Table 15. Basic syllable statistics

	Isol. consonant. microsegment		One-phon. syll.	Two-phon. syll.	Three-phon. syll.	Four-phon. syll.	Five-phon. syll.	Six-phon. syll.	Seven-phon. syll.	Eight-phon. syll.	Total
	one-phon.	two-phon.									
Russian.											
Distinct Syllables	12*	3*	8	319	1991	638	55	3	0	0	3029
Running Syllables	1088	40	2564	23654	13743	1733	156	3	0	0	42981
Czech											
Distinct Syllables	6*	2*	8	297	1596	659	64	5	0	0	2637
Running Syllables	975	51	1963	23864	12464	2670	220	10	0	0	42217
German											
Distinct Syllables	0	0	14	270	938	888	332	67	5	1	2515
Running Syllables	0	0	870	12498	17820	4817	1131	147	5	1	37289

* Corresponding voiced and voiceless consonants of Russian and Czech, and palatalized and non-palatalized consonants of Russian, constituting isolated consonantal microsegments, as well as /š/ and /ž/ which can occur in Russian as isolated consonantal microsegments in certain environments, are counted separately in this table.

in the use of the system, then symbols most likely to occur in actual messages should require the least time and/or energy in the transmission (depending on the kind of efficiency which concerned us), while longer symbols should be assigned only to communicative units of lesser probability. This principle is certainly intuitively plausible; information theory procedures supply a formal proof of the requirement.

If the three natural languages investigated here follow to some extent the principle of efficiency as far as syllable use is concerned, then we would expect this to be manifested by a tendency for the relative frequency of a syllable in actual messages to be inversely proportionate to its length: the longer the syllable, the smaller its frequency of occurrence should be. If this is true, on the average, then the ratios of running syllables to distinct syllables in each of our corpora should *decrease* as the syllable length increases. Table 16 lists these ratios.

Table 16.—Ratios of running syllables to distinct syllables

	Russian	*Czech*	*German*
1-phoneme syllables*	182.60	209.86	62.14
2-phoneme syllables**	73.58	79.98	46.29
3-phoneme syllables	6.90	7.81	19.00
4-phoneme syllables	2.72	4.05	5.42
5-phoneme syllables	2.84	3.44	3.41
6-phoneme syllables	1.00	2.00	2.19
7-phoneme syllables	—	—	1.00
8-phoneme syllables	—	—	1.00

* including 1-phoneme isolated consonantal microsegments.
** including 2-phoneme isolated consonantal microsegments.

These ratios represent the *average* frequency of a syllable of the respective type, not the actual frequency of any particular syllable.

The figures in Table 16 indeed show that the ratio generally decreases with syllable length in all three languages. However, the rate of decrease is much more gradual in German than in the Slavic languages. This already suggests a conclusion — which will be confirmed later in this chapter by a more rigorous calculation — that the coding efficiency of German, as far as syllable use is concerned, is noticeably less than that of Russian or Czech.

The general tendency to minimize the cost of transmission of symbols in language messages, displayed here for syllables, holds with some additional limitations also for the frequency distribution of words. On the whole, the longer the word, the smaller its frequency of occurrence is likely to be. This property of natural languages has been extensively studied (by Zipf, 1935 and 1949; Miller and Newman, 1958; Mandelbrot, 1961; and others). A detailed discussion of the possible linguistic significance of the observable tendency toward some minimization of cost in the transmission of language messages is beyond the scope of this study. Our investigation of syllable distribution also reveals such a general tendency but suggests, at the same time, that considerable differences exist among various languages within this general economy pattern — differences which may turn out to be of more linguistic interest than the general overall similarity.

The figures displayed in Table 16 should not be taken as demonstrating that the frequency distribution of syllables in any of the three languages is the optimal one. There are, in each language, specific syllables which have a higher occurrence frequency than specific shorter syllables. Theoretically, therefore, the communicational efficiency of each system could be improved by reassigning certain syllables to different "words".

The constraints on the sequence of phonemes within the syllable work against economy. The consequence of these constraints is the expansion of the syllable inventory by syllables which are longer than would be necessary under optimal conditions. If there were no restrictions whatsoever on the structure of the syllable (i.e. all possible sequences of segmental phonemes could constitute a legitimate syllable), only one-, two-, and three-phoneme syllables would be needed in any language. In Russian, for example, where the largest number of segmental phonemes is available, such lack of constraints would give a set of 70,643 different syllables of one to three phonemes in length.

The absence of any constraints on syllabic structure is, of course, an unrealistic assumption because the very definition of the phonological syllable (and the possibility of delimiting it in the utterance) depends on the presence of a syllabic nucleus. This, in itself, already implies a constraint on the structure of the string. However, even with the addition of the limitation that every syllable must contain a nucleus consisting of a vowel, one- to three-phoneme syllables would still be sufficient. There would be 26,672 different syllables of this kind in Russian, for example.

Comparing the average length of the syllable in the three corpora is also instructive in considering the phonological structure of the three languages. The first figure in Table 17 gives the average length in phonemes of a syllable in the "syllable dictionary" compiled from the corpus, i.e. the average length of a syllable regardless of frequency of occurrence. The values for Russian and Czech are very close to each other but the German figure is considerably higher. The second set of figures indicates the average length of the running syllable in the text, computed simply by dividing the total number of phonemes in each corpus by the total number of running syllables. Again, the Russian and Czech figures are very similar, the German one significantly higher.

Table 17.—Average length of syllable in phonemes

	Russian	*Czech*	*German*
Distinct syllables	3.1304	3.1820	3.5885
Running syllables	2.3266	2.3687	2.8205

The first row of figures points out that the average length of the German syllable, based on the dictionary of syllables, is approximately 113% that of the Czech and 115% of the Russian syllable length. The second row shows that these differences increase in the running syllables. The length of the German running syllable is approximately 119% of that of the Czech and about 121% of the length of the Russian syllable.

Both these sets of figures thus indicate again that German, on the average, has longer syllables than the two Slavic languages do and that, in actual utterances, the longer syllables are used with a proportionately greater frequency in German than in Russian or Czech. We shall see later the interesting consequences of this difference in the computation of entropy based on the syllable as a unit of analysis.

It may be of interest to compare the syllable length figures in Russian, Czech and German with the figures for English which can be extrapolated from the results of the statistical phonological analysis of American English reported by Roberts (1965, pp. 44 and 113–117). Such a comparison can be made, of course, only with reservations. The material on which Roberts' analysis is based is substantially different from ours (compiled from word-frequency lists rather than from running texts) and Roberts gives no rigorous definition of the syllable. Nevertheless, a general comparison is possible.

Interestingly enough, the extrapolation from Roberts' figures shows that the average length of the running syllable in English (i.e. taking the relative frequencies of syllable occurrence into account) is 2.7695 phonemes, which is substantially higher than in Russian or in Czech and only slightly below the figure obtained by us for German. Roberts does not give the number of different syllables and of their types by length, so that no other comparisons can be made.

Because of the differences in the type of data and in analytic procedures, only a cautious conclusion is possible. Nevertheless, it can be said that English utilizes shorter syllables proportionately less than Russian or Czech do and that English resembles German in this respect. This would indicate that the efficiency of use of syllables in English utterances is lower than in Russian and in Czech, but comparable to or slightly higher than in German.

Such simple statistical indicators as the average length of syllables do not, however, give much more than the most general indication about syllable structuring. It must be remembered that each of the languages being compared here has a different number of segmental phonemes, a factor which must be taken into consideration before any more definite statements about the "efficiency" of syllable structuring and use can be made. This problem is dealt with in the next section.

5.2. Entropy as a Comparative Indicator of Syllabic Structure

Syllables are phonological units and the range of their function in signalling linguistic meaning in actual messages varies widely. In the case of mono-syllabic microsegments, the syllable may be coextensive with a "word" and may signal both semantic meaning and grammatical relations. In polysyllabic words, these functions are performed by sequences of syllables which are subject to additional constraints. An examination of our data indicates that the constraints on syllable sequences within polysyllabic microsegments are substantial. A further discussion of the combinatory properties of syllables within larger segments can be found in Chapter 7.

The pronounced sequential restrictions on syllable combinations only emphasize the point that the investigation of the structure and communicative efficiency of syllables is by no means equivalent to the determination of the overall entropy and redundancy of the language.

Languages are organized hierarchically, with words composed of syllables, sentences of words, and continuous discourse being an assemblage of sentences, many of which are grammatically and semantically interdependent. But language communication is not a simple concatenation of smaller units into larger ones; rather it is a complex process of building messages according to a "grammar", an underlying set of abstract relationships which the native speaker of a language learns in childhood, perhaps in the form of subconscious or semi-conscious rules. It can therefore be shown (as has been done by Chomsky and his followers repeatedly) that a model of language which would attempt to explain linguistic messages as strings of symbols, generated linearly according to certain probabilities, cannot provide an adequate basis for a general linguistic theory. It should be added, however, that Chomsky's proof of the inadequacy of elementary finite-state grammars does not necessarily exclude the possibility of constructing a more complex probabilistic model of linguistic communication which could prove adequate.

In any event, it is certainly possible to analyze some of the units of language (such as syllables) by procedures applicable only to finite-state systems. This section of the monograph is intended to demonstrate that useful insights into linguistic structuring can be gained by the application of such procedures, principally of those derived from the mathematical theory of communication.

5.21. Basic Assumptions of Communication Theory

The continuum of speech has always been analyzed by linguists as a series of discrete symbols. Even when some procedures of speech analysis result in an iconic representation (such as a speech sonogram, for example), linguistics proceeds to restate this kind of gradient image of speech in digital terms, as a chain of separate segments each analyzable even further (for example, into binary distinctive features). This digitalization of speech in linguistic study reflects, without much doubt, the intuitive approach to language by humans who seem to handle naturally the encoding and decoding of messages as a manipulation of discrete symbols.

Communication theory presupposes — in the case of discrete systems — that the transmission of information can be represented as a discrete stochastic process. The communicational source produces a series of symbols according to certain probabilities. These symbols, chosen from a finite set (usually referred to as the *alphabet* of the source) are independent events in some communication systems; in that case, the occurrence probability of a particular symbol is not affected by the symbols which precede it in the message. In other systems, the probability that a particular symbol is chosen depends on the state of the source, i.e. on the configuration of those symbols of the message that have already been produced. A simple but revealing example from written English illustrates a system in which the probabilities of individual symbols depend on the state of the source. The overall occurrence probability of the grapheme *u* in English is approximately 0.025 (see Hultzén, 1964, p. 1). However, if the letter *q* had just been generated, *u* is certain to be the next symbol (if one excludes such marginal instances as Qantas Airlines). This simply reflects the requirements of English orthography. The probability of *u* varies depending on the state of the system: in a post-*q* state its probability is one, and in other states less than one.

This latter type of stochastic process is known technically as a discrete

Markov chain. The term Markov chain refers, in a narrow sense, to stochastic processes in which the probability of an event depends at most upon the event immediately preceding. But the concept can be extended by viewing the communication process in terms of a finite number of possible states of the system, with a set of transitional probabilities specifying that the system will proceed from a given state to another state. A state can then be defined as a sequence of symbols of any needed length, already produced in the message.

The assumptions of communication theory and the fact that natural languages cannot adequately be described by simple finite-state grammars imply certain limitations on the use of communication theory procedures in language analysis. Such a communicational analysis of language can be either an analysis of a system which is an approximation to the language in question or, alternatively, must be limited to certain subsystems of language. The latter approach is utilized in this chapter.

Unlike sentences, syllables can be described by a finite-state grammar. This is possible in principle because phonological syllables in any language have a maximum specifiable length, in phonemes, and the set of different well-formed syllables is therefore finite. It is, moreover, advantageous to analyze syllables by such finite-state procedures because the most revealing constraints operative within syllables involve neighboring phonemes and phoneme groups.

The basic notion of communication theory is the concept of information as a function of the number of alternatives which are possible when the communication source is in a given state. This concept of information is independent of any consideration of semantic meaning in the conventional sense; information theory procedures are not intended to measure the profundity or triviality of the message, nor its behavioral consequences.

The theory proceeds from the assumption — which is certainly intuitively plausible — that if no alternative is possible in the communication process, then no uncertainty exists as to the occurrence of the next symbol to be produced in the message and that, consequently, no information is transmitted by such a predictable symbol. In our English graphic example, in which the probability of *u* after *q* is one, no information is transmitted by the letter *u* in this state.

A Russian phonemic example can further illustrate the principle: assuming that the two phonemes /+ms'/ have been generated in a post-disjuncture onset, the next two phonemes are predictably /t'í/ and therefore transmit no information. This example is not intended, of course, to be a description of actual speech perception which very likely is not a strictly linear decoding process but rather a recognition of configurations larger than phonemes. It is possible that a linearly redundant phoneme may thus contribute significantly to language decoding.

The Russian phonemic example also illustrates some applications of communication theory in the analysis of syllabic structures. As was pointed out, in the Russian syllable /+ ms't'íl+/ 'he took revenge' (which is also a phonological word) two phonemes, /t'/ and /í/ are predictable in a left-to-right syllable generation. The vowel /í/ serves as a syllabic nucleus and thus performs a configurative function. The phoneme /t'/, however, could be omitted without any loss of information. This Russian word is then, at the very least, longer by one phoneme than it needs to be. The amount of this type of "redundancy" in coding can be measured by communication theory procedures.

On the other hand, the greater the uncertainty as to the choice among the various symbols, the more average information is transmitted per symbol. Uncertainty as to choice among symbols depends on two variables. First of all, uncertainty increases as the number of different symbols in the alphabet of the system increases. In a communication system with only two symbols, both equally likely to occur, the guess as to the symbol transmitted next can be made with an average accuracy of fifty percent. In a system with four different equiprobable symbols, the accuracy of the guess would be no better, on the average, than twenty-five percent, and so on.

The other variable of uncertainty in the choice of symbols is the probability distribution of the occurrence of the symbols. The higher the probability of a given symbol, the less surprise value it has in the message. Again, let us consider a simple communication system with only two symbols, a and b, where a is, on the average, nine times as frequent as b. In guessing the next symbol to be produced by this source, a consistent prediction of a should be correct nine out of ten times, on the average. This improvement of the guessing performance over a comparable system where both symbols have equal occurrence probability indicates that the average uncertainty per symbol of the second system is considerably less than in the first one. The notion of uncertainty of choice then logically leads to the assignment of less informational capacity to a source which utilizes symbols with highly varied probabilities than to one with more nearly equiprobable symbols. This consideration is obviously important in practice because most communication systems (including natural languages) employ symbols which are not equiprobable.

As was already pointed out briefly in Section 5.1, the total efficiency of a communication system is also a function of the relationship between the probability of the symbol and the time and/or energy required for its transmission. If the aim is coding efficiency as to time, then more frequent symbols should be shorter and should require less transmission time than less frequent ones.

The average rate of information transmitted per symbol-unit is measured by the familiar formula developed by Shannon for discrete noiseless systems (Shannon and Weaver, 1949):

$$H = -K \sum_{i=1}^{n} p_i \log_2 p_i \qquad \text{(F1)}$$

where K is a constant which simply amounts to the choice of a measuring unit of the information rate. If information is being measured in binary units (*bits*) and the logarithm is to the base 2, then $K = 1$.

The sum is taken over all distinct symbols of the alphabet of the source which have the probability distribution p_1 to p_n. H is then said to be the *entropy* (in bits per symbol) of such a source. The formula is applicable if the symbol occurrences are independent events.

As can be seen from formula (F1), the average information rate will reach its maximum value if all symbols are equiprobable. This is so because, in the special case of equiprobability, all values of p_i will be equal to $1/n$, where n is the number of different symbols in the system. (F1) then simplifies to

$$H = -\sum_{i=1}^{n} p_i \log_2 p_i$$

$$= -n \cdot \frac{1}{n} \cdot \log_2 \frac{1}{n}$$

$$= \log_2 n \qquad \text{(F2)}$$

Since the number of different symbols in the alphabet of a source is one of the factors in the uncertainty being measured, entropy H is not directly comparable for systems employing different numbers of distinct symbols. Therefore, it is desirable to compute the relative entropy H_{rel} as the ratio of H to the maximum entropy which the source could have, provided only that it utilized the same symbols but with equal probabilities. This gives:

$$H_{rel} = \frac{H}{H_{max}}$$

$$= \frac{-\sum\limits_{i=1}^{n} p_i \log_2 p_i}{\log_2 n} \tag{F3}$$

which is independent of the number of symbols n. The value of H_{rel}, being a ratio of actual to maximum entropy, will always be between zero and one. $1 - H_{rel}$ is the *redundancy R* of the source, commonly expressed as a percentage.

If we consider, for the time being, segmental phonemes to be independent events with stable probabilities, then the entropy and redundancy for the phoneme probability distributions in Russian, Czech, and German can be computed by applying the above formulas to the figures given in Table 4. The simplification assumed in this case, in which no restrictions on sequences of phonemes are taken into account, is generally known as a first-order approximation.

Calculating in this manner, we obtain the following values (rounded to four decimal places):

$$Russian \quad H_1 = 4.8257 \text{ bits/phoneme}$$
$$Czech \quad H_1 = 4.7006 \text{ bits/phoneme}$$
$$German \quad H_1 = 4.4435 \text{ bits/phoneme}$$

The maximum entropy H_{max} is the average entropy per segmental phoneme which a system could have if it used all phonemes with equal probabilities. As shown in (F2), H_{max} is equal to the logarithm to the base 2 of the number of phonemes in the language, i.e.

$$Russian \quad H_{max} = \log_2 41 = 5.3576 \text{ bits/phoneme}$$
$$Czech \quad H_{max} = \log_2 35 = 5.1293 \text{ bits/phoneme}$$
$$German \quad H_{max} = \log_2 33 = 5.0444 \text{ bits/phoneme}$$

The relative entropy values H_1/H_{max} are:

$$Russian \quad H_{rel} = 0.9007$$
$$Czech \quad H_{rel} = 0.9164$$
$$German \quad H_{rel} = 0.8809$$

and the redundancy of the systems $(1 - H_{rel})$

$$Russian \quad R = 0.0993 \quad or \quad 9.93\%$$
$$Czech \quad R = 0.0836 \quad or \quad 8.36\%$$
$$German \quad R = 0.1191 \quad or \quad 11.91\%$$

For comparison, it may be of interest to list two sets of figures obtained for English in two separate projects. The first entropy calculation was made by Roberts (1965, p. 395) from a large body of data obtained in a phonemic analysis of Horn's word-frequency list of English. Roberts operates with an inventory of 32 phonemes. The second set of figures comes from the book of Hultzén et al. (1964, p. 29). The latter calculation was based on a corpus of 20,032 running phonemes (originally assembled by John B. Carroll) and on an English phonemic system of 43 phonemes, including juncture:

English		Roberts	Hultzén
H_1	=	4.4947	4.64
H_{rel}	=	0.8989	0.85
R	=	0.1011 or 10.11%	0.15 or 15%

The redundancy figures obtained by this method reflect solely the non-equiprobability of segmental phonemes. No constraints on phoneme sequences have been included in the calculation, and this drastic simplification makes such results of limited value.

Nevertheless, the differences in the redundancy figures among the four languages are of some interest because they represent a quantitative summary of the probability distributions of segmental phonemes in each language as a whole.

The ranking of four languages in order of increasing redundancy, i.e. Czech, Russian, English (as reported by Roberts), and German, shows no discernible correlation with the number of segmental phonemes. It is true, of course, that H_{rel} and R, which essentially measure the degree of deviation from the theoretical equiprobable distribution of phonemes, are mathematically independent of the number of different phonemes employed in the language. However, the study of some other statistical properties of languages, especially of vocabulary, suggests that, in practice, various elements of language may be affected in their frequency distribution by the number of distinct element-types employed in the communication process.

In the study of vocabulary usage in English, for example, it has been found that the frequency distribution of word-types (i.e. different words utilized in the communication) deviates increasingly from the theoretically possible equiprobable distribution of such types as the number of types becomes larger (for details see Kučera and Francis, 1967, and Kučera, 1968). This holds for distributions in the range from 500 and 50,000 word-types (about 2000 to 1 million running words), and quite probably for larger vocabularies as well.

The probability distributions of segmental phonemes show no clear tendency to be affected by the number of distinct phonemes in the languages analyzed here. In our case, Czech, with the lowest redundancy, has 35 phonemes, followed in redundancy by Russian with 41 phonemes. Only then comes English which has (in Roberts' interpretation) the lowest number of phonemes, 32; the highest redundancy is found in German with only 33 phonemes.

The probability distributions of phonemes in several languages and the frequency distribution of word-types in one language may not be comparable. Nevertheless, it is useful to point out the statistical differences of the two types of distributions, precisely in order to emphasize that the statistical properties of various elements of language have to be interpreted in terms of the function of these elements and cannot be viewed simply as a by-product of those properties of language which are accounted for by some random function and are, therefore, of little linguistic interest.

Phonemes are not linguistic signs, i.e. they do not signal meaningful entities, but simply serve as differential elements in distinguishing meaning. Words, on the other hand, are linguistic signs which generally refer to cognitive entities. Word frequencies can thus be expected to be affected more directly than phonemes by the repeat rate with which certain concepts and relationships need to be communicated in language messages. This kind of correlation between the function of linguistic elements and their statistical properties requires, of course, further investigation.

Also of some interest is the fact that the Hultzén computation of H_1 for English, which is based on the largest number of phonemes of all the languages, namely 43, gives by far the highest redundancy value. The expansion of the phonemic inventory in the Hultzén analysis, as compared to Roberts' system, thus resulted in a higher degree of skewness of the probability distribution of English phonemes. But this may have multiple causes (such as introduction of marginal phonemes of low frequencies or the inclusion of juncture in the alphabet of the system) and no generalization can be made on the basis of this single piece of evidence.

5.22. Entropy Calculations Based on the Syllable as Unit of Analysis

The average entropy per phoneme computed in Section 5.21 does not, of course, offer any information on the comparative structure of the syllables in the analyzed languages. In order to obtain information of this kind, a different calculation must be made.

As was already demonstrated, phoneme occurrences cannot be considered to be independent events because the occurrence probability of a phoneme depends on the state of the source. Since we are interested in the analysis of the syllable, the occurrence probabilities of individual phonemes within the syllable can be considered to depend on the phonemes already generated in the respective syllable.

For our purposes, we shall make the simplification that syllables are independent events but that the phonemes which compose syllables are subject to sequential restrictions. We shall attempt to measure the overall degree of these restrictions in each language. At the same time, we shall be interested in measuring the efficiency with which syllables of comparable structures are utilized in message composition in the three languages.

We are thus dealing with a source which produces syllables composed of phonemes whose probabilities of occurrence depend on the state of the system in the syllable generation process. This requires, first of all, that the set of all possible states of the system in the generation of the syllable be ascertained and that the occurrence probability of each state be estimated. In each state, of course, the probability of certain phonemes will be different, and some phonemes will not occur at all, i.e. will have a zero probability. For example, if the syllable generating system is in a post-/r/ state (having generated as the first phoneme /r/), then there is a zero probability in all three languages of /l/ being produced next. On the other hand, if the system is in a post-/š/ state (having generated /š/ as the first phoneme of the syllable) then there is a non-zero probability, in any of our three languages, that /l/ may be the next symbol.

It is thus necessary to determine, for each state, the set of possible phonemes and their probabilities. For each state i there is a set of probabilities $p_i(j)$ of the system producing the various symbols j. Consequently, it will be possible to compute the entropy H_i for each state of the system.

The probability that a particular state will be reached in syllable generation is unequal for the various possible syllable states. We can see from the data presented previously (in Table 15, for example) that the probability of the syllable generation continuing up to the sixth phoneme (before the syllable is terminated) is very small although non-zero in each of the three languages.

But the unequal probability of the states is not only a matter of syllable length. Syllables composed of certain phoneme sequences will be employed much less frequently in actual messages than syllables of the same length but containing other phoneme configurations; these differences in occurrence frequencies will then be reflected in the probabilities assigned to various states in a sequential syllable generation model.

In order to take the unequal likelihood of occurrence of different states of the generating system into account, the total entropy of the source which we are considering will be defined as the sum of all H_i (that is, entropies of individual states) weighted in each case by the probability P_i of the occurrence of the state:

$$H_s = \sum_i P_i H_i$$

$$= - \sum_{i,j} P_i \, p_i(j) \log_2 p_i(j) \qquad \text{(F4)}$$

where the sum is taken over all i states and over all j phonemes.

In order to compute H_s according to formula (F4), the syllables in our project had to be ordered in a specific way, for each language separately.

Every distinct syllable was first assigned its probability of occurrence which was estimated by dividing the frequency of a particular syllable by the total frequency of all syllables in the respective corpus. The syllables, left-justified and with their estimated probabilities attached, were then computer sorted in an ascending order so that all syllables beginning with the same phoneme were grouped together regardless of length. Syllables beginning with two identical phonemes occupied adjacent positions in a subgroup, and so on. In essence, this ordering amounted to the alphabetization of the syllables.

Syllables consisting of eight phonemes were the longest retrieved from any of the three corpora; they occur in German only. The longest syllables in Russian and in Czech attested in our data are six phonemes in length. In order to illustrate the organization of the data and to facilitate further discussion, the following scheme can be used to represent the syllables as ordered for the computation.

In this scheme, the letter S represents a syllable slot filled by a phoneme and the numeric subscript the position of the slot in the syllable, counting from left to right; the alphabetic subscripts, using the letters from a to z, are general symbols for the phonemes occupying the position, each letter representing a different phoneme. The ordered syllable set, with attached probabilities, can then be represented as follows:

Syllable	Probability
S_{1a}	$p(S_{1a})$
$S_{1a}S_{2a}$	$p(S_{1a}S_{2a})$
$S_{1a}S_{2a}S_{3a}$	$p(S_{1a}S_{2a}S_{3a})$
.	.
.	.
.	.
$S_{1a}S_{2b}$	$p(S_{1a}S_{2b})$
$S_{1a}S_{2b}S_{3a}$	$p(S_{1a}S_{2b}S_{3a})$
.	.
.	.
.	.
S_{1b}	$p(S_{1b})$
$S_{1b}S_{2a}$	$p(S_{1b}S_{2a})$
.	.
.	.
.	.
$S_{1z}S_{2z}S_{3z}S_{4z}S_{5z}S_{6z}S_{7z}S_{8z}$	$p(S_{1z}S_{2z}S_{3z}S_{4z}S_{5z}S_{6z}S_{7z}S_{8z})$

The average entropy per phoneme was computed by a generalized IBM 7070 program applicable to all three languages. The number of possible states for S_1, that is, the number of phonemes which can begin a syllable (S_{1a}, S_{1b}, S_{1c} ... S_{1z}) was first determined and the occurrence probability of each different phoneme in S_1 calculated. This allowed the computation of the average entropy H_1 per phoneme for state S_1. In this special case, the probability of a given phoneme in S_1 is simply equal to the probability that a syllable will begin with that phoneme.

The number of different states in which the system can be after the first syllable phoneme has been produced is equal to the number of different phonemes in S_1. This means that, using our notation, S_{1a} represents a different state of the system from S_{1b}, etc. For each S_1, it was thus necessary to determine the phonemes which can occur in S_2 and compute their probabilities. The entropy for the various S_2 states could then be computed, by summing the product of the probability of each phoneme in that state and of the logarithm of the probability. Each such state entropy had to be weighted by the overall probability of the state's occurrence.

The program then proceeded to the next position, S_3. This time, there were as many different states to be considered as there were different two-phoneme syllable beginnings. Again, entropy was calculated for each state, and the program proceeded to the next position.

A blank, which signals the end of a syllable, was considered to be the final state of the syllable and was included as such in the entropy calculations. Once the end of a syllable was detected in this manner, the particular syllable was eliminated from subsequent calculations.

The following average entropy results were obtained by our calculation (rounded to four decimal places):

$$Russian \quad H_s = 2.7024 \text{ bits/phoneme}$$
$$Czech \quad H_s = 2.6541 \text{ bits/phoneme}$$
$$German \quad H_s = 2.3618 \text{ bits/phoneme}$$

In order to compare the three results, we need to eliminate from the comparison the factor due to the different number of segmental phonemes employed by each language. We thus calculate the relative entropy H_{rel} as the ratio of H_s/H_{max} (where H_{max}, in this case, is calculated on the basis of the phoneme set plus the signal of the syllable end):

$$Russian \quad H_{rel} = 0.5012$$
$$Czech \quad H_{rel} = 0.5134$$
$$German \quad H_{rel} = 0.4642$$

Redundancy $(1 - H_{rel})$ calculations give:

$$Russian \quad R = 0.4988 \quad \text{or } 49.88\%$$
$$Czech \quad R = 0.4866 \quad \text{or } 48.66\%$$
$$German \quad R = 0.5358 \quad \text{or } 53.58\%$$

The difference in the redundancy values between the Slavic languages and German is readily apparent. The Czech redundancy figure is only about 91 % of the German, the Russian one approximately 93 % of the German value.

This warrants the general conclusion that, on the basis of our data, the efficiency of the phonemic structuring and use of the syllable is noticeably higher in the Slavic languages, especially in Czech, than it is in German. As will be recalled, this conclusion was anticipated earlier in this chapter when the syllable length and the ratios of running to distinct syllables in the three languages were compared. However, the rigorous entropy calculations have made it possible to state the structural differences among the three languages in terms of precise quantitative values. It also makes a similar future comparison with still other languages feasible.

As was the case in the calculation of relative entropy and redundancy based on the probability distribution of segmental phonemes in the language as a whole, no discernible correlation between the number of phonemes and redundancy is apparent in the syllable-based calculations either. It should also be mentioned that there is no evidence that the number of vowel phonemes (which are the principal ingredients of the required syllabic nucleus) is a factor in the communicational properties of syllables. German, with the highest syllable-based redundancy, has also the largest number of vowel phonemes (14, compared to 10 in Czech and 8 in Russian) and, therefore, the best theoretical possibility of generating the largest number of distinct syllables, at least as far as the shorter syllables are concerned.

As large as our redundancy values are, they do not represent, of course, the total redundancy of the language on the phonemic level. In our analysis, syllables were treated as independent events, and none of the constraints which limit the admissibility of certain syllable sequences in the formation of larger units (microsegments or words) have been taken into account.

Additional constraints, absolute or probabilistic, on sequences of higher-level linguistic units, which are imposed by the requirements of morphology and syntax, have been disregarded in our calculations as well. Chapter 7 of this book examines certain types of constraints operative within larger-than-syllable units and discusses these restrictions in the framework of the overall linguistic structure.

5.23. Typological Implications

With only three languages analyzed, one cannot do much more than speculate whether the difference in redundancy values between the Slavic languages and German has any relationship to the more highly inflected structure of Russian and of Czech, as opposed to the less inflected German.

Although several redundancy estimates for various languages have been published in the literature, they are mostly rough estimates only and do not offer any reliable indication whether the overall redundancy is approximately the same in all natural languages or whether it may vary significantly from language to language. Our results do not necessarily prove that redundancy varies in different languages. It is entirely conceivable, although this remains to be tested, that Russian and Czech may impose greater restrictions than German does on sequences of syllables or larger units, and thus end up eventually with a total redundancy similar to that of German. In highly inflected languages, a relatively small set of syllables representing inflectional suffixes occurs with high frequency and relatively high predictability (and, therefore, high redundancy).[10] One could thus speculate that such a factor might increase the total redundancy of Russian and of Czech so that it approximates the overall redundancy of the less inflected German. However, since other factors obviously enter into the picture (such as constraints on sequences of article plus following word in German), any such conclusions have to await further investigation. If it could be shown in subsequent research that syllabic redundancy, as computed here, correlates inversely with the degree of inflection of a language, this observation may offer a useful criterion in typological classifications.

The similarity of the redundancy values between Russian and Czech, two closely related languages genetically, is also of interest. It supports the observation, apparent also from phonotactics, that Russian and Czech have a very similar syllabic structure, in spite of their rather dissimilar inventory of phonemes and the substantial differences in their employment of distinctive features. This would seem to suggest that syllabic structure is a relatively stable element in the diachronic profile of a language and is not very greatly affected, at least in general terms, by prosodic and other differences in the phonological systems of closely related languages (see also Chapter 6). In this case too, of course, a larger number of genetically related languages would have to be examined before any reliable generalizations could be made.

5.24. Some Other Methods of Entropy Calculation

As far as we know, the calculation of entropy and redundancy, described in the preceding section, represents the first utilization of this particular method in the comparative analysis of the structure of a linguistic unit. However, some other procedures of communication theory were employed before by other researchers in linguistic analysis.

Previous uses of communication theory in linguistics had a different aim from ours. Our purpose was the quantitative comparison of the phoneme composition and use of syllables in several languages. Our main interest was thus in the structure of a functional unit of language. Previous informational studies, on the other hand, usually had as their aim an approximate determination of the overall entropy and redundancy of a language. Strictly

---

10 An interesting example of this type of restriction has been pointed out by Jakobson with regard to the small number of phonemes which are utilized in the case endings of Russian nouns (see Jakobson, 1958, p. 142).

speaking, an accurate calculation of the entropy of a natural language is impossible because languages are not finite-state systems. The only realistic aim in attempting to estimate the entropy of a language is, therefore, a satisfactory approximation.

The most commonly used procedure in such approximations has been to base the calculation on phoneme or grapheme blocks of fixed length and to make entropy estimates by taking into account the observed segmental constraints in phoneme or grapheme digrams, trigrams or even longer strings.

In a recent report on the phonemic sequences of English (Hultzén, 1964), entropy values are computed on the basis of estimates obtained from four-phoneme sequences. The material for the Hultzén study was the phonemically transcribed corpus of American English originally assembled by John B. Carroll, which contains 20,032 running phonemes. Since the phonemic transcription and subsequent computations were based on an inventory of 43 phonemes (including juncture), $H_{max} = \log_2 43 = 5.43$. The entropy calculations were done according to the formula

$$H = - \sum_{i,j} p(i,j) \log_2 p_i(j) \qquad (F5)$$

where i is a prior state of the system and j any following state, $p(i,j)$ the probability of the joint occurrence of the two states, and $p_i(j)$ the transitional probability of j following when i occurs.

It can be seen that this formula, when applied to phoneme sequences, is similar to our procedure but that it will calculate the entropy value on the basis of restrictions on phoneme occurrences within phoneme blocks of fixed lengths. In contrast to this, the constraints on phoneme occurrences taken into consideration in our computation were those operative within blocks of variable length as represented by the non-arbitrary linguistic unit of the syllable.

In Table 18, based on the results reported in the Hultzén book, entropy values are given for four levels. In level 1, only the overall probabilities of phonemes were considered, with no sequential constraints. In level 2, restrictions observed within sequences of two phonemes entered into the calculation, in level 3 those of three phonemes, and in level 4 four-phoneme sequences were considered.

If we use Roberts' figure specifying the average length of the English syllable as 2.7695 phonemes (remembering, of course, that Roberts uses a somewhat different phonemic system) then we might expect, on the basis of the Hultzén results, that the entropy calculated for English syllables would be

Table 18.—Entropy estimates for English (according to Hultzén)

Level	H	H_{rel}	R
1	4.64	0.85	15%
2	3.47	0.64	36%
3	2.42	0.45	55%
4	1.65	0.30	70%

roughly 2.66 bits per phoneme. This, in terms of Hultzén's phonemization, would point to a redundancy of some 49%, which seems a realistic figure if compared with our calculation for other languages. However, this kind of extrapolation from the Roberts and Hultzén calculations has to be taken with a grain of salt for several reasons. First of all, the Roberts and the Hultzén phonemic systems of English are different. Secondly, the Carroll corpus, on which the Hultzén figures are based, is probably much too small to make reliable estimates of the probability of four-phoneme sequences possible. And finally, and most important, our assumption that the entropy computed for syllables is roughly the same as the entropy computed for phoneme blocks of fixed length, equal in number of phonemes to the average length of the syllable, may be unwarranted. Since the nature of the constraints on phoneme sequences changes with syllable type, the averaging procedure could lead to substantial distortions. Only actual calculations for the English syllable could answer the question of how significant this distortion might be.

The approximation procedure used by Hultzén (and by other researchers as well) has certain serious drawbacks from a linguistic point of view. The segmentation of the phonemic string into blocks of fixed length raises, among others, the question whether configurational entities, such as word boundaries or junctures, should or should not be considered to be members of the joint event whose probability is being determined. But a more serious disadvantage is the simple fact that the aim of this kind of approach is not the investigation of functional linguistic units (such as syllables or microsegments) but rather an estimate of the overall entropy of the language, which from the linguistic point of view is something of a futile aim, to begin with.

Another shortcut method was used by Shannon in calculating the average entropy of English graphemes within word boundaries (Shannon, 1951). By taking certain known properties of word-frequency distributions into consideration, Shannon was able to calculate the approximate probability distribution of words in actual English texts and thus obtain the average entropy per graphic word. Dividing this value by the average number of letters in an English word, he then calculated the average entropy per letter.

We tried a similar method on our data, in order to see how different the results would be from those obtained in our principal calculation.

The distinct syllables retrieved from each set of data were considered to be the alphabet of the system and their probability of occurrence was estimated from our corpora. To obtain the entropy values for phonemes, the entropy in bits/syllable was divided by the average number of phonemes constituting a syllable in the respective language. This calculation yielded the following results:

Table 19.—Entropy estimates based on syllable frequencies

	H bits/syll.	H_{rel} for syllables	H bits/phoneme	H_{rel} for phonemes	R for phonemes
Russian	8.9942	0.7777	3.8658	0.7216	27.84%
Czech	8.9416	0.7868	3.7749	0.7359	26.41%
German	9.0359	0.7991	3.2037	0.6351	36.49%

As far as the results obtained for phonemes are concerned, the substantially higher entropy values and, consequently, redundancy figures of only little over one-half of those obtained by our principal method, are not surprising. This alternate procedure simply treats all the distinct syllables of the corpus as the alphabet of the system and then computes entropy in terms of the probability distribution of these syllables, regardless of syllable composition or length. This amounts to the same thing as assuming that all syllables are of the same (i.e. average) length but occur with different probabilities. The restrictions on phoneme sequences within the syllable enter into the calculation only indirectly, in the form of the limitation on the number of distinct syllables assumed in the system. The degree of efficiency of syllable use as to length is not a factor in such a calculation at all.

Nevertheless, the comparison of our principal method and the approximation given here is not without interest. We can gain from it some indication of the fraction of the overall redundancy accounted for by the specific constraints operative in syllables of different types, and of the fraction accounted for by the probability distribution of syllables of different lengths.

The difference between the phoneme redundancy values for German and for the Slavic languages is striking. It is proportionally even greater than that obtained in our principal calculation. This time, the redundancy of Czech is only 72% of the German value, and that of Russian 76% of the German figure.

On the other hand, entropy H for syllables is slightly higher in German than in the Slavic languages, despite the fact that German has the smallest number of distinct syllables of the three languages (2515, compared to 3029 in Russian, 2637 in Czech). It means that the actual probability distribution of syllables in German deviates less from the optimal equiprobable distribution than is the case in Russian or in Czech. This can also be seen from the fact that German has the highest relative entropy for syllables. The high phoneme redundancy of German obtained in this calculation is thus due to the fact that the average length in phonemes of the German syllable is considerably greater than that of Czech or Russian syllables. This greater average length reflects, if only indirectly, the greater degree of constraint on phoneme permutations admissible within the German syllable.

As we have already emphasized before, even the relatively high redundancy figures of around 50%, obtained by our principal method, do not represent the "overall" redundancy of the analyzed languages. Taking the constraints on sequences of syllables into account would obviously increase the redundancy figures quite substantially, as the calculations in Chapter 7 suggest. In general, our results again point out that realistic redundancy estimates for natural languages need to be quite high, certainly well over 50%.

In linguistic literature, a number of estimates of redundancy for various languages can be found. Most of such approximations refer to graphemes rather than to phonemes and are often based on not entirely reliable experimental procedures. Such redundancy estimates appear to range between 50–80% (for some references, see Jaglom *et al.*, 1960).

Chapter 6

PHONEMIC ISOTOPY AND
LANGUAGE DIVERGENCE

The average entropy per phoneme calculated in the preceding chapter for phonemes within syllable boundaries offered some general quantitative indications of the overall structural properties of syllables in the three languages and of the "efficiency" in the use of syllables in message generation.

The similarity between the Russian and the Czech results, compared to the higher redundancy results for German, suggests that the more similar patterning of syllables in the two Slavic languages may reflect their closer genetic relationship to each other as contrasted with their more distant relationship to German. But the results of the entropy calculations cannot be considered, by themselves, to demonstrate such a conclusion. It is conceivable that two languages, genetically unrelated and having entirely different inventories of phonemes and, consequently, different syllable strings, may yield identical or very similar values in the calculation of entropy for phonemes within syllables. This is so because the entropy determination is based only on a probability distribution of a set of symbols (phonemes, in this case) in the various states of the systems, but does not at all take into account any other properties of the symbols, such as — in our case — the phonetic properties and the degree of phonological similarity of the symbol sets in the compared languages.

In considering two or more languages as being similar in terms of phonological patterns (for example, for the purposes of discerning behind such similarity the genetic relationship between them) linguists certainly would consider not only probability distributions (although these, too, enter into the picture indirectly), but also, and primarily, actual phonological similarity of the segments which compose the similarly patterned strings.

The measurements of phonemic isotopy and of language divergence described in this chapter are intended to take into account these additional factors which are relevant to the estimation of the overall degree of similarity of two phonological systems. As will be demonstrated, these additional variables need to be both quantitative and qualitative, very much as even the impressionistic linguistic judgments of the "similarity" of two systems are both qualitative and quantitative. The statement that two languages resemble each other in syllabic structure and use would most probably mean to the linguist that, in actual language messages, syllables of similar phoneme composition occur with somewhat similar frequencies.

The Isotopy Index which was developed by Henry Kučera (1964) is designed to measure the approximate degree with which phonologically similar strings (in our case syllables) occur with similar frequencies in two languages. One may expect that the degree of similarity, defined in this manner, will show some correlation with the degree of genetic relationship of the two languages as reflected on the phonological level.

Three key concepts in the computation of the Isotopy Index need to be explained: syllabic position, isotopy, and isomorphy.

Syllabic position

Syllabic position is the place of a phoneme defined both in relation to the nucleus and in relation to the boundaries of the syllable. The notation used in this study and defined in Chapter 4 (for example the symbol O_{31}) defines such an exact position within a syllable. The basic relationship to the nucleus is specified by the letter symbol (O = onset, that is a position to the left of the nucleus, while C = coda would indicate a position to the right of the nucleus) and, more precisely, by the second subscript digit (in our case, the subscript value of one designates the position immediately preceding the nucleus). The position relative to the syllable boundaries is indicated by the first subscript digit. In our example, O_{31}, the first subscript digit indicates that the specific onset contains three filled positions which means that the position next to the nucleus must also be the third position from the beginning of the syllable.

Each position can be filled by a specific set of phonemes, constituting the membership of the position, and the probability of each phoneme in any given syllabic position can be estimated from the sample. The phoneme memberships and the frequencies of individual phonemes for each possible syllabic position were given in Tables 12, 13, and 14.

Isotopy

Two phonemes which can occur in identical distributional positions in two languages (in our case, in identical syllabic positions) are said to be isotopic. In our approach, isotopy will be considered more significant the closer the probabilities of occurrence of these two phonemes in the comparable syllabic positions.

Isomorphy

The concept of isotopy would be without much practical significance for the comparison of two languages if there were no procedure available for determining which particular phonemes from the two languages should be compared in a given position. It is for this reason that the final computation of the Isotopy Index must include some qualitative indication of the degree of phonological proximity of each group of phonemes being compared.

The comparison of phonemes of two different languages thus requires a measure of their phonemic similarity which is referred to here as the measure of isomorphy and designated by M. This measure is based on the matrix of distinctive features operative in the two systems. The fewer the number of distinctive features in which the corresponding phonemes differ, the greater M will be. The isomorphy measure, which is explained in detail later in connection with the derivation of the Isotopy Index, may have values from zero (no isomorphy) to one (identity).

In his recent book, Gustav Herdan (1964, pp. 50–56), in discussing Kučera's Isotopy Index, points out that the isotopy measure as originally proposed includes both quantitative and qualitative criteria, i.e. that both isotopic and isomorphic values enter into the final calculation. Herdan considers this fact to be a shortcoming of the method. This criticism is based on a misunderstanding of the nature of phonemes.

In our view, a phoneme is a class of sounds identifiable by a common set of distinctive feature values. While distinctive features are presumably universal and the set of features used by natural languages not only finite but quite small, distinctive features are relative, i.e. they are not absolute qualities but oppositions, identifiable only by analyzing the structure of a particular language.

Given this view of the phoneme, it is not possible to say simply that we shall compare identical or "similar" phonemes of two different languages as to their occurrence in a given syllabic position. The identity or the similarity of the two sets of sounds which we call phonemes in two languages has to be rigorously defined, not simply assumed or vaguely guessed. It is for this reason that the measure of isomorphy is necessary, not only for grouping phonemes for purposes of comparison, but also to indicate quantitatively what weight any particular comparison should have in the total calculation.

Moreover, if there were no procedure available for determining some kind of phonological isomorphy, then there would ultimately be no way of grouping for comparison those phonemes in the two languages which have no clear-cut counterparts in the other phonological system. How would one determine, for example, with which Czech vowel the German /ö/ should be compared in the calculation? Surely, the phoneme /ö/ cannot be entirely disregarded; but neither can it be completely arbitrarily assigned to a group, let us say, with Czech /e/ or, alternatively, to a group with Czech /o/, or to some other set. Only a rigorous and linguistically justifiable procedure can lead to consistent and meaningful decisions in the treatment of those phonemes which have no obvious counterparts in the other system. As will be seen, the isomorphy concept used in this study provides such a procedure.

6.1. Calculation of the Isotopy Index

The frequency of occurrence of each phoneme in each syllabic position in our corpora was retrieved with the aid of a computer program and the respective probabilities thus estimated. Since three languages were being compared, provisions had to be made for the maximum number of syllabic positions which occur in any of the three corpora. This included a total of 26 positions designated, in our notation, as:

Nucleus positions:	N
	$N_1 \ N_2$
Onset positions:	O_{11}
	$O_{22} \ O_{21}$
	$O_{33} \ O_{32} \ O_{31}$
	$O_{44} \ O_{43} \ O_{42} \ O_{41}$
Coda positions:	C_{11}
	$C_{21} \ C_{22}$
	$C_{31} \ C_{32} \ C_{33}$
	$C_{41} \ C_{42} \ C_{43} \ C_{44}$
Isol. cons. micro-segment positions:	I_1
	$I_{22} \ I_{21}$

In a number of instances, the frequency of all phonemes of a language in a certain position was zero. In Czech, for example, no four position codas exist and therefore the frequency of any Czech phoneme in positions C_{41}, C_{42}, C_{43}, C_{44} will be zero. The same is true in Russian in relation to N_1 and N_2, of German in relation to isolated consonantal microsegment positions, or of German with reference to four-position onsets. In addition to that, many phonemes do not occur at all in some position slots and their probability for that particular syllabic position is thus recorded as zero.

The phonemes of each pair of languages being compared were grouped into isomorphic sets in such a way that the resulting sets had the maximum possible isomorphy. The underlying principle of this grouping was the phonological analysis based on distinctive features. The distinctive feature matrices of the two languages were compared and all those phonemes were first grouped into isomorphic sets which, in both matrices, had identical feature specifications. This principle creates, for example, the following completely isomorphic sets:

Russian /c/ and Czech /c/ which are both non-vocalic, consonantal, non-compact, non-grave (which is the consonant feature of high tonality), non-nasal, non-continuous, and strident.

Czech /p/ and German /p/ which are both non-vocalic, consonantal, non-compact, grave, non-nasal, non-continuous, and voiceless.

Russian /š/ and German /š/, both specified as non-vocalic, consonantal, compact, acute (which is the consonant feature of high tonality), non-nasal, continuous, and voiceless.

Those phonemes which could not be fitted into completely isomorphic sets were grouped with those phonemes of the other language from which they differed by the smallest number of distinctive features. This principle sometimes resulted in the grouping, in a single isomorphic set, of more than one phoneme of one language with a single phoneme of the other language. For example, Russian /b/ and /b'/ and Czech /b/ constitute an isomorphic set; all three are non-vocalic, consonantal, non-compact, grave, non-nasal, non-continuous, and voiced. But the Russian /b/ and /b'/ are also differentiated as plain *vs.* sharp, i.e. by a feature which is not employed in Czech.

In order to take into account the degree of similarity of those phonemes grouped into isomorphic sets, the measure of isomorphy M was computed as

$$M = \left(1 - \frac{d}{f}\right) \tag{F6}$$

where d is the number of features in which the phoneme or phonemes of the first language differ from the phoneme or phonemes of the second language within a given isomorphic set. The denominator f is the maximum number of features needed to define that phoneme, in either of the two languages under comparison, which requires the largest number of distinctive features (not counting zeros) for its identification (see distinctive feature Tables 1, 2, and 3). It should be borne in mind that f is not necessarily the total number of distinctive features found in either matrix, nor is it necessarily the number of features needed to define the specific phoneme for which M is being computed. Rather f is equal to the largest number of plus and minus signs found in any single column of either of the two compared matrices. Once f has been determined for a pair of languages, it remains constant in the computation of M for all isomorphic sets.

From the distinctive feature matrices in Chapter 3, it can be seen that, in Russian, the phonemes requiring the largest number of features for their identification (which includes most consonants) are specified by eight feature values. In Czech, the largest number of features is required to specify /t/, /d/, /ţ/ and /ḑ/, — eight features each. In German, the largest number of features needed to identify any phoneme is seven, which is the case in a large number of phonemes (all of the obstruents and most of the front vowels). Thus, in comparing Russian and Czech, f will equal eight; in the Russian-German comparison, f equals eight (the larger of the two numbers needed to specify a phoneme in either of these two languages), and in the Czech-German computation, f is also equal to eight.

If we apply the formula for determining M to some actual cases, we will find that in all completely isomorphic sets (such as Russian /c/ and Czech /c/, Czech /p/ and German /p/, or Russian /š/ and German /š/, and others) M equals unity. This is so, because, in these cases,

$$M = 1 - \frac{0}{f} = 1$$

regardless of the value of f.

However, for sets which are not completely isomorphic, M will be less than one. To return to our previous example, for the set consisting of Russian /b/ and /b'/ and of Czech /b/ we have

$$M = 1 - \frac{1}{8} = 0.875$$

This is the case because either one of the two Russian phonemes of the isomorphic set requires for its identification the feature sharp vs. plain, while the Czech phoneme does not have this feature. Thus, d in this case is equal to one.

Another example from Czech and German may further illustrate the rather frequent situation in which one phoneme of the first language has to be grouped with two phonemes of the other language. Let us first assume that the Czech short /e/ is grouped with both the German /e/ and /ö/. The Czech phoneme and both German phonemes have the following features in common: they are vocalic, non-consonantal, non-compact, non-diffuse, non-grave, and short. These are all the features needed to specify the Czech vowel. However, the two German vowels also require identification as to the feature flat vs. non-flat: /e/ is non-flat, and /ö/ is flat. Thus, again, d in this case equals one, while f for the Czech-German pair is eight, so that for this particular isomorphic set we have

$$M = 1 - \frac{1}{8} = 0.875$$

While the Czech /e/ and the German /e/ could be rather easily grouped into an isomorphic set, as can the Czech /o/ and the German /o/, the problem arises because of the German phoneme /ö/ which has no obvious counterpart in the Czech system. As far as /ö/ is concerned, an alternative organization of isomorphic sets would be to group both the German /o/ and /ö/ with the Czech /o/. All three phonemes are vocalic, non-consonantal, non-compact, non-diffuse, and short. However, while /o/ in both languages is grave, /ö/ is non-grave. Moreover, /ö/ also must be identified as flat, a feature which is not needed in the specification of either the Czech or the German /o/. There are thus two feature differences among Czech /o/, German /o/ and German /ö/, and d = 2. Therefore,

$$M = 1 - \frac{2}{8} = 0.750$$

which is a smaller value than that obtained for M in the first grouping (Czech /e/, German /e/, German /ö/). Since the criterion for assigning phonemes to isomorphic sets is the achievement of the largest possible values of M (i.e. the greatest possible isomorphy), the first solution for the German /ö/ has been adopted in our calculation.

If a distinctive feature is suspended in certain distributional positions (as the voiced vs. voiceless opposition in certain final consonants before external and terminal disjuncture in all three languages, or the feature sharp vs. plain in some consonants in certain clusters in Russian) this fact has been taken into consideration in the computation of M and the suspended feature has not been included in the calculation of the respective d.

In those few instances when an equally high value of M could be obtained by two different isomorphic groupings, our choice was based on distributional criteria. For example, the Czech palatal /ţ/ can be grouped either with the Russian palatalized /t'/ or the non-palatalized /t/; in either case, $d = 2$. An inspection of Tables 12 and 13 will show that Czech /ţ/ displays greater distributional similarity with Russian /t'/ than with Russian /t/, in such matters as the syllabic positions which these phonemes occupy. Other distributional properties of the two languages reinforce this observation.

For these reasons, we grouped the non-grave voiceless non-continuants into two isomorphic sets, the first containing Russian /t/ and Czech /t/, the second composed of Russian /t'/ and Czech /ţ/. These groupings are also in good agreement with the facts of historical phonology of the Slavic languages.

Table 20 lists the isomorphic sets of phonemes which we used in the calculations of the Isotopy Index for the three language pairs.

Table 20.—Isomorphic sets of phonemes

Russian — Czech		Russian — German		Czech — German	
p p′	p	p p′	p	p	p
b b′	b	b b′	b	b	b
t	t	t t′	t	t ţ	t
t′	ţ	d d′	d	d ḑ	d
d	d	k k′	k	k	k
d′	ḑ	g	g	g	g
k k′	k	f f′	f	f	f
g	g	v v′	v	v	v
f f′	f	s s′ c	s	s c	s
v v′	v	z z′	z	z	z
s s′	s	š č	š	š č	š
z z′	z	ž	ž	ž	ž
š	š	x	x h	x	x
ž	ž	m m′	m	h	h
x	x h	n n′	n ŋ	m	m
c	c	l l′	l	n ŋ	n ŋ
č	č	r r′	r	l	l
m m′	m	i í j	i i:	r ř	r
n	n	é	e e:	i j	i ü
n′	ŋ	a á	a a:	i:	i: ü:
l l′	l	ó	o o: ö ö:	e	e ö
r	r	u ú	u u: ü ü:	e:	e: ö:
r′	ř			a	a
j	j			a:	a:
i í	i i:			o	o
é	e e:			o:	o:
a á	a a:			u	u
ó	o o:			u:	u:
u ú	u u:				

In each isomorphic set, the phonemes were then assigned their occurrence probabilities separately for each syllabic position. These probabilities were estimated from our corpora. In those cases when more than one phoneme from a language had to be included in a single isomorphic set, the phoneme probabilities were summed. For example, in syllabic position O_{11}, the Russian /p/ has the occurrence probability 0.01357, Russian /p′/ 0.00428, and Czech /p/ the probability 0.01605. In assigning the probabilities for the syllabic position O_{11} to the isomorphic set consisting of the Russian /p/ + /p′/ and Czech /p/, the two probabilities for Russian were summed, so that the Russian side now had the total probability of (p + p′) = 0.01785, the Czech subset simply the probability of /p/, namely 0.01605.

The *Isotopy Index* for a pair of languages A and B is then computed as

$$I = \sum_{i=1}^{n} \frac{p_i(A) \cdot p_i(B)}{\left[\dfrac{p_i(A) + p_i(B)}{2}\right]^2} \cdot \frac{p_i(A) + p_i(B)}{2} \cdot M_i$$

$$= \sum_{i=1}^{n} \frac{2p_i(A) \cdot p_i(B) \cdot M_i}{p_i(A) + p_i(B)} \tag{F7}$$

The calculation of the Index takes into consideration the occurrence probability of every isomorphic set in every syllabic position in which any element of the respective isomorphic set occurs. The value of n is thus equal to the total number of isomorphic sets represented with non-zero probability in all syllabic positions in either of the two compared languages. Consequently, $\sum_{i=1}^{n} p_i(A) = \sum_{i=1}^{n} p_i(B) = 1$. The actual values of n used in our calculations are given in Section 6.2.

As can be seen from the formula (F7), the Isotopy Index I depends on three factors:

a) One factor is the isomorphy measure M as determined for each isomorphic set. As has been shown previously, M can have values from zero to one. In comparing completely isomorphic phoneme sets, M will have no effect on the computation, since $M = 1$. If phonemes were to be compared which did not share any distinctive feature specifications, then $M = 0$ and the particular term of the sum would be also zero. However, since our aim is to group into isomorphic sets only those phonemes of the two languages which have as much isomorphy as possible, the case of $M = 0$ is unlikely to arise in practice.

b) The value of I depends further on the difference between the probability of the corresponding phoneme or phonemes in language A and language B in the respective syllabic position. In (F7) the expression

$$\frac{p_i(A) \cdot p_i(B)}{\left[\dfrac{p_i(A) + p_i(B)}{2}\right]^2}$$

will reach its maximum value of one if and only if $p(A)$ and $p(B)$ are equal, i.e. when the corresponding phonemes occur with equal probability in both languages in the comparable syllabic position. The value of the expression will decrease as the difference between $p(A)$ and $p(B)$ increases and reach zero when either one of the probability values is zero. As specified above, only those syllabic positions are considered in the calculation of I in which at least one of the elements of the respective isomorphic set occurs. The case of both $p_i(A)$ and $p_i(B)$ having zero values thus does not arise.

c) Finally, I depends on the average probability with which any of the phonemes composing the isomorphic set are encountered in the comparison of the two languages in the given syllabic position. This is expressed as the ratio of the summed probabilities of the phonemes of a given isomorphic set in the respective syllabic position to the sum of all the phoneme probabilities in the first language (which is, of course, one) plus the sum of probabilities of all phonemes in the second language (which is also one), i.e. on the ratio of the summed probabilities to two. The greater this ratio, the greater the effect which the isomorphic set in the particular syllabic position will have on the value of I. Since the Isotopy Index is intended to measure the degree of *overall* phonological similarity in the structuring and use of language units (syllables, in our case), obviously greater weight should be given to the degree of similarity or lack of it which is evidenced in frequently occurring syllabic positions than to those positions which occur rarely. The Isotopy Index computation accomplishes this by weighting the result for each isomorphic set in a specific syllabic position by the average probability in this syllabic position of the phonemes composing the set, which is expressed as

$$\frac{p_i(A) + p_i(B)}{2}$$

If the two languages under comparison were identical in syllable composition and use, then the Index would equal unity. This would be the case because all values of M would be equal to one (all phoneme sets being completely isomorphic) and the expression

$$\frac{p_i(A) \cdot p_i(B)}{\left[\dfrac{p_i(A) + p_i(B)}{2}\right]^2}$$

would also give the result of one for each value of i, since the probabilities of the corresponding phonemes in every syllabic position would be the same in language A and language B. This reduces the Index to the expression

$$\sum_{i=1}^{n} \frac{p_i(A) + p_i(B)}{2}$$

which by definition is one, being the sum of the probabilities of all phonemes in all syllabic positions in the two languages (equal to two) divided by two.

6.2. Isotopy Indices of Russian/Czech, Russian/German, and Czech/German

The value of n in (F7) is obtained by determining the total number of isomorphic sets represented in all syllabic positions in either of the two compared languages. In our study, the following values were obtained for n (with the relevant distinctive feature suspensions in certain syllabic positions taken into account): for Russian/Czech, $n = 243$; for Russian/German, $n = 183$; and for Czech/German, $n = 195$.

If the occurrence probability of an isomorphic set is non-zero in one but zero in the other of the compared languages, then the isomorphic set in this particular syllabic position contributes a zero value to the Isotopy Index. In actuality, therefore, the number of non-zero terms accounting for the value of I is smaller than n. In our calculations, the number of isomorphic sets with non-zero probability for a given syllabic position in both languages (i.e. the number of non-zero terms comprising I) was as follows: for Russian/ Czech, 159; for Russian/German, 102; and for Czech/German, 101.

The following are the values of I obtained for the three language pairs:

$$Russian/Czech \quad I = 0.75957650$$
$$Russian/German \quad I = 0.47411752$$
$$Czech/German \quad I = 0.61638397$$

The three results clearly show, at least for the languages under consideration here, that the Isotopy Index correlates well with the degree of genetic and typological relationship. Not only does the Russian/Czech Index have the highest value, indicating the correlation with the degree of genetic relationship, but the Czech/German Index is substantially higher than the Russian/German Index, well in accord with the non-quantitative linguistic evidence of the closer Czech/German phonological "similarity" in comparison to the Russian/German situation.

The Isotopy Index is, of course, a purely relative measure and the interpretation of the values obtained in its calculation is not easily possible with only a few available results. The usefulness of I or of some refined version of the Index as a typological indicator or as a potential tool of historical research can be assessed better only after it has been applied to a larger number of language pairs. In addition to this, several calculations of the Index on different corpora of phonological data for the same language pair would also be desirable so that the statistical characteristics of the Index could be more precisely determined.

6.3. Language Divergence and Its Components

Herdan discusses Kučera's first published proposal of the Isotopy Index in considerable detail in his recent book (Herdan, 1964, pp. 50–56). Among other things, Herdan shows that if the isomorphy measure M is disregarded in the computation of the Index (or set equal to unity, which is the same thing), the Index can be simplified to

$$I = \sum_{i=1}^{n} 2 \left(\frac{1}{p_i(A)} + \frac{1}{p_i(B)} \right)^{-1} \qquad \text{(F8)}$$

which is the sum of the harmonic means of the probabilities for the (completely) isomorphic set i.

Herdan then adduces the proof that the Isotopy Index is indeed a suitable measure of the extent of similarity or discrepancy between the probabilities of isomorphic phonemes, with limiting values of one for complete identity and zero for complete dissimilarity.

In Herdan's book, a simpler computation of the Isotopy Index is also proposed which, however, is suitable only for two samples of equal size and applicable only if degrees of isomorphy are disregarded:

$$I = \frac{2}{N} \sum_{1}^{n} \left(\frac{1}{n_1} + \frac{1}{n_2} \right)^{-1} \qquad \text{(F9)}$$

where n_1 and n_2 are the frequencies of occurrence rather than the probabilities of the phonemes in the respective syllabic position and N is the size of each sample.

The complete elimination of M which Herdan proposes is — as was already pointed out — linguistically unacceptable. Nevertheless, Herdan's criticism that Kučera's Isotopy Index does not reveal what proportion of the Index value is due to isomorphy (i.e. phonological similarity among the phonemes of the two languages) and how much to isotopy proper (i.e. distributional and probabilistic phonological properties) is valid. In order to eliminate this uncertainty, we performed another calculation on the same data with the single difference that all phoneme sets were considered to be completely isomorphic, i.e. M was assumed to be equal to one in all calculations.

In the following summary, I designates the original Index value and J the modified value (computed with M set equal to one).

Table 21.—Unmodified and modified Isotopy Indices

	I	J	$(J - I)$
Russian/Czech	0.75957650	0.90891796	0.14934146
Russian/German	0.47411752	0.69178206	0.21766454
Czech/German	0.61638397	0.73797250	0.12158853

In order to make the relative roles of the qualitative and quantitative factors clearer, let us introduce the concept of Language Divergence D, defined simply as

$$D = 1 - I \tag{F10}$$

The total value of D can be accounted for by the factor d_m which is due to incomplete isomorphy of the compared phonemes, and by d_t which is due to the isotopic factor proper, i.e. differences in the distribution and statistical properties of the compared phonological systems. We thus have

$$D = d_t + d_m \tag{F11}$$

where $d_t = 1 - J$, and $d_m = J - I$.

Table 22 gives the values of d_t, d_m and D for each language pair. The last column lists the ratio of d_t to d_m.

Table 22.—The components of Language Divergence

	d_t	d_m	D	d_t/d_m
Russian/Czech	0.09108204	0.14934146	0.24042350	0.61
Russian/German	0.30821794	0.21766454	0.52588248	1.42
Czech/German	0.26202750	0.12158853	0.38361603	2.16

The results given in Table 22 point out the substantial differences in the Divergence values for the three language pairs. D for Russian/German is 2.2 times greater, and D for Czech/German 1.6 times greater than the values of D computed for the Russian/Czech pair. Of considerable interest for the evaluation of the language comparison are the relative contributions of d_t and d_m in the three sets of results. The Divergence fraction due to isotopy proper, i.e. d_t, is quite small in the Russian/Czech analysis but quite significant in the comparison of the Slavic languages with German. Table 22 shows that d_t for Russian/German is 3.4 times greater, and d_t for Czech/German 2.9 times greater than d_t for Russian/Czech. On the other hand, the Divergence fractions due to incomplete isomorphy show no comparable correlation with the degree of genetic relationship. The lowest value of d_m is found in the Czech/German comparison; d_m for Russian/Czech is only slightly larger but d_m for Russian/German almost twice as large as the isomorphy fraction of D for Czech/German. This difference in the contribution of the two factors to the overall Language Divergence values becomes even clearer if the percentages of D which are due to d_t and d_m in the three sets of results are specified.

For Russian/Czech, d_t constitutes 37.5% and d_m 62.5% of the total Language Divergence. For Russian/German, the relative contribution is roughly reversed, d_t accounting for 58.6% and d_m for 41.4% of D. And finally, the Czech/German comparison shows that d_t constitutes 68.3% and d_m only 31.7% of the total value of D. In considering these results, the reader should bear in mind that the absolute value of d_m is smaller for Czech/German than for the more closely genetically related Russian/Czech pair.

All these results warrant the conclusion that — as far as the three languages analyzed here are concerned — the phonological similarity between genetically closely related languages is largely a matter of distributional and quantitative properties of phonemes, i.e. of *quantitative phonotactics*, rather than a matter of close correspondences between the phonemic inventories of such languages. If this conclusion can be substantiated in the analysis of other language pairs, our method could be utilized not only to measure the degree of phonological similarity but perhaps also as a discovery procedure in establishing the probability of genetic relationship between two languages.[11]

---

[11] Greenberg (1957) discusses a number of methodological problems in formulating hypotheses of genetic relationship among languages. In relation to the necessity of eliminating chance in such comparative considerations, Greenberg says: "The most straightforward method of eliminating chance would be the calculation of the expected number of chance resemblances between two languages, taking into account their respective phonemic structures. In practice, this proves extremely difficult, and no satisfactory technique for its accomplishment has yet been devised. Moreover, it requires, in addition to consideration of the possibilities of phonemic combination, a frequency weighting of phonemes." (Greenberg, 1957, p. 37.)

Although our quantitative comparative method does not proceed directly from the establishment of the expected number of chance resemblances, it would appear to meet Greenberg's basic requirements for a suitable measure of genetic relationship.

Chapter 7
SYLLABLE SEQUENCES

Since the primary aim of all the preceding calculations was the comparative study of syllable structuring and use, the quantitative procedures employed so far have been based on the concept of the syllable as a statistically independent event, and all restrictions which the language systems impose on sequences of syllables have been disregarded. Given our main objective, this was a justifiable simplification.

Empirically it is obvious, however, that syllables are not independent events and that every language has some restrictions, absolute as well as probabilistic, as to which syllables may or may not follow each other. The quantitative determination of the extent of these constraints is even more complex than the investigation of phonological restrictions within syllables. Only some aspects of this problem are examined in this chapter. Although results are reported here only for Russian, where we carried our research farther than in the other two languages, it may be assumed that rather similar types of constraints are operative in Czech and in German as well.

Tables 23 and 24 present information about the phoneme and syllable composition of microsegments in the Russian corpus. It will be recalled that a microsegment (defined in Chapter 4) represents, in our analysis, the next higher phonological unit after the syllable. All the tables in this chapter are based on the entire Russian corpus (not on a dictionary compiled from the corpus); the frequency figures thus refer to running microsegments and to running syllables.

Although the Russian corpus consists of exactly 100,000 phonemes, the last phoneme represents the beginning of an incomplete microsegment (as well as of an incomplete syllable) and is thus not included in the count in Table 23.

In addition to the information summarized in Tables 23 and 24, the Russian corpus was also analyzed for the number of sequences of two syllables. There are altogether 8,142 different sequences of two syllables in the corpus (referred to further as two-syllable *types*) which account for a total of 20,893 occurrences of two-syllable sequences (referred to as two-syllable *tokens*). It should be emphasized that only those sequences of two successive syllables were taken into consideration, in this count, which occurred without inter-

Table 23.—Phoneme composition of microsegments in the Russian corpus

Length of microsegment in phonemes	Number of microsegments of given length	Number of corpus phonemes accounted for by microsegments of given length
1	1378	1378
1 (isol. cons. microsegments)	1088	1088
2	3806	6612
2 (isol. cons. microsegments)	40	80
3	2998	8994
4	2472	9888
5	2922	14610
6	2430	14580
7	1933	13531
8	1202	9616
9	788	7092
10	453	4530
11	275	3025
12	139	1668
13	76	988
14	38	532
15	30	450
16	9	144
17	7	119
18	2	36
19	2	38
Total	22088	99999

Average length of microsegment = 4.5273 phonemes

Table 24.—Syllable composition of microsegments in the Russian corpus

Length of microsegment in syllables	Number of microsegments of given length	Number of corpus syllables accounted for by microsegments of given length
1	8380	8380
2	6846	13692
3	3818	11454
4	1418	5672
5	375	1875
6	93	558
7	20	140
8	8	64
9	2	18
Isolated cons. microsegments	1128	1128
Total	22088	42981

Average length of microsegment = 1.9459 syllables

ruption by a disjuncture. The analysis is thus based only on two-syllable sequences found within a microsegment, not on syllables belonging to two different microsegments.

In considering these figures, the reader should bear in mind that a microsegment consisting of two syllables yields one two-syllable sequence, a microsegment of three syllables yields two two-syllable sequences (first + second syllable, and second + third syllable), etc. In general, a microsegment of n syllables yields $n - 1$ two-syllable sequences.

Let us now consider the design of a communication system which could produce a text transmitting the same information as our Russian corpus but which would encode this information more efficiently. In other words, the task is to recode the Russian corpus with the objective of minimizing the total number of phonemes which compose it without interfering with the information carrying capacity of the text.

The data available in the various tables will aid us in this task, although the information contained in them is not quite sufficient for arriving at an optimal system of recoding. In order to accomplish such an optimal recoding, we would need to have additional data at our disposal, such as a complete frequency distribution table of all microsegments.

For our limited purposes we shall simply assume that we will duplicate the Russian corpus as far as isolated consonantal microsegments and all other monosyllabic microsegments are concerned. Our recoding will be limited to polysyllabic microsegments only. We know from Table 15 that we have available in Russian (disregarding isolated consonantal microsegments) 8 distinct one-phoneme syllables, 319 different two-phoneme syllables, 1991 different three-phoneme syllables, etc. Working only with this syllable inventory but admitting all possible two-syllable sequences without any restrictions, we could get $8 \times 8 = 64$ different two-syllable types of two phonemes in length, $8 \times 319 + 319 \times 8 = 5104$ two-syllable types of three phonemes in length, $319 \times 319 + 8 \times 1991 + 1991 \times 8 = 133{,}617$ two-syllable types of four phonemes, and so on.

Even such a simple calculation convincingly shows that no sequence of two syllables in the corpus has to be longer than four phonemes, since only 8,142 two-syllable types are needed. It also follows that the maximum length of any syllable occurring in a polysyllabic microsegment does not need to exceed two phonemes and that the average length of such a syllable can be estimated at 1.68 phonemes (provided that we make the simplified — and from our point of view unfavorable — assumption that all two-syllable types have the same relative frequency of occurrence). Even with this partial and very elementary recoding principle, we could shorten the Russian corpus substantially. No change in monosyllabic and isolated consonantal micro-segments and no change in the overall syllable composition of the corpus is effected in this recoding.

Table 25.—Partially recoded Russian corpus

Microsegment type	No. of syllables (incl. isol. cons. microsegments)	No. of Phonemes
Isolated consonantal microsegments	1128	1168 (= Russian corpus)
Monosyllabic microsegments	8380	18228 (= Russian corpus)
Other microsegments	33473	56235 (recoded)
Total	42981	75631

Since the original Russian corpus as analyzed for microsegments contained 99,999 phonemes (see Table 23), the partial recoding has saved 24,368 phonemes, i.e. reduced the corpus size by about 24%. This saving was accomplished simply by removing the restrictions on sequences of two syllables within microsegments which had accounted for this additional redundancy of the text.

A further substantial reduction in the length of the corpus would become possible with the availability of additional information about the statistical properties of the text. Since our aim is the minimization of the size of the corpus in terms of total number of phonemes, the best strategy would obviously be to assign the shortest possible syllables and syllable sequences to those microsegment-types which have a high frequency of occurrence, leaving the longer syllables for microsegments of low frequencies.

The requirement in the recoding exercise that the information-carrying capacity of the text should not be reduced is not inconsequential from a linguistic point of view. We interpreted this requirement as equivalent to the condition that the number of two-syllable types has to remain the same in order for the text to retain the same signalling properties. However, since all possible two-syllable sequences have been permitted in the recoding, the resulting communication code would be in all probability quite different from a natural language. The new code — unlike a natural language — could not systematically signal linguistically important relationships by designating semantically related morphemes with similar syllable sequences. Nor could such a code utilize syllables to form systematic patterns of grammatical morphemes as effectively as natural languages do. This only demonstrates again that the investigation of overall redundancy in natural languages may be of general theoretical or specific typological interest but that the results can hardly serve as the basis of any kind of value judgment about the total "inefficiency" of language.

Chapter 8

CONCLUSION

The exposition and the calculations in this monograph have aimed at demonstrating, first of all, that certain mathematical procedures applicable to finite state communication systems can be useful in linguistic analysis, provided that such a study is concerned with specific and well-defined properties of natural languages. Procedures of information theory can be employed with advantage, for example, in the comparative study of the structure of certain subsyntactic elements, such as morphemes or syllables, and the results of a quantitative comparison of this kind can be expected to offer insights not only into some aspects of the phonotactics of a language but also into more general problems of linguistic typology. The calculations of the Isotopy Index in Chapter 6 and the specification of the components in such an estimate of phonological similarity of two languages point out the possibility of identifying the basic parameters of the phonological manifestation of genetic relationship.

The choice of the phonological syllable as our basic unit of analysis resulted from several considerations. As we tried to demonstrate in Chapter 4, the syllable can be delimited consistently by hierarchical segmentation of the utterance and by an application of ordered rules in a manner which gives satisfactory results for the three languages of interest to us and appears applicable to other languages as well. The phonological syllable is a unit displaying with sufficient scope the combinatory properties of phonemes, characteristic of a given language, and thus offers a suitable basis for the contrastive study of phonotactics of several languages. At the same time, the phonological syllable is a small enough segment for the purposes of quantitative study of language. The total inventory of different syllables, retrieved from a corpus of manageable size, is not so large as to prevent the possibility of useful estimates of the relative frequency of various syllabic structures.

The Russian, Czech and German corpora were selected so as to be comparable in content and style. The phonemic transcription of Russian and Czech was completely automatic and that of German semi-automatic. The use of computer processing in the transcription and the analysis of the data

103

(originally intended primarily as a time-saving device) assured the consistency of the transcription procedure and the elimination of errors in subsequent calculations.

The consistent delimitation of the phonological syllable in the three languages made it possible, first of all, to conduct a comparative study of the phonemic structures of the syllables in the three languages and to determine the overall degree of constraint which is the consequence of the admission of only certain sequences of phonemes in the formation of syllables. Already, elementary quantitative results give an indication of the relative phoneme utilization in syllable formation in the three languages. The tendency of German to use a higher proportion of longer syllables than either of the Slavic languages suggests immediately that more severe constraints on phoneme sequences within syllables may be operative in German. More precise calculations, such as the entropy determination at the syllable level described in detail in Chapter 5, verify this guess. While the redundancy of German, calculated by taking sequential constraints on phonemes within syllables into account, amounts to 53.58%, the redundancy for Russian is only 49.88%, and that of Czech is the lowest, 48.66%.

Two sets of tentative conclusions can be drawn from the entropy results:

a) Redundancy figures show that the degree of constraint is smaller (and, conversely, the phonotactic "efficiency" greater) within the syllables of the two Slavic languages than it is for German. Additional calculations, presented in Chapter 5, point out one other important fact. The entropy in bits per syllable is highest in German, as is the value of relative entropy calculated for the syllable as the basic symbol of the source (see Table 19). Consequently, the redundancy of German, calculated for syllable units, is lower than in either Russian or Czech. This is of interest because it shows that the probability distribution of the syllables in German is closer to the optimal distribution in terms of information theory (i.e. to an equiprobable distribution) than is the case in the two Slavic languages. The fact that German, in spite of this more favorable probability distribution of syllables, has a significantly higher redundancy in calculations using the phoneme as the basic symbol of the source, points out even more strikingly that the higher redundancy of German is due to greater constraints on phoneme sequences in syllable formation and to more frequent use of longer syllables, but not to the probability distribution of syllables as such in actual utterances.

b) The closeness of the entropy and redundancy results for the two Slavic languages warrants the tentative suggestion that the similar degree of constraint may reflect similar principles of phonotactics in these two genetically closely related languages. This conclusion is confirmed in the calculations of the components of the Isotopy Index, presented in Chapter 6.

Strictly speaking, similar results in entropy and redundancy calculations do not necessarily warrant the conclusion that the two systems have similar phonotactics. The entropy determination is based only on a probability distribution of a set of symbols (phonemes in our case) in the various states of the source, but it does not take into account at all any qualitative properties of the symbols, such as the phonological characteristics of the symbol sets in the individual languages. It is thus conceivable that two languages, having entirely different inventories of phonemes and different syllable strings, might yield identical or similar values in the calculation of entropy and redundancy for phonemes within syllables. The determination of the Isotopy Index, presented in Chapter 6, introduces the necessary qualitative phonological considerations into the comparison.

The Isotopy Index consists of two components, isotopy proper and isomorphy. Isotopy proper measures, essentially, the similarity of phonotactics in two languages, calculated in terms of the probability distribution of matched phonemes in corresponding syllabic positions. Isomorphy, on the other hand, measures the degree of qualitative similarity of the phonemes matched in the calculation. Since the overall Isotopy Index includes both of these factors, a high value of the Index (which has the limits of zero and one) may be due either to significant isomorphy or to significant isotopy proper, or to both factors. Conversely, a low Isotopy Index value can be accounted for by substantial differences in the inventory of phonemes (i.e. the isomorphy factor) or by phonotactic dissimilarities (i.e. by isotopy proper).

In order to isolate the relative role of these two factors in the Isotopy Index, Chapter 6 includes calculations of both the isomorphy component and the component of isotopy proper for each language pair. To make the results of the language comparisons more revealing, the concept of Language Divergence is introduced. The measure of Language Divergence D is defined simply as the difference between the actual Isotopy Index and the maximum possible value of the Index, which is unity (i.e. $D = 1 - I$).

The Language Divergence value is, as one might expect, lowest for the Russian/Czech pair. It is higher for the German/Czech pair, and highest for the Russian/German pair. However, an analysis of the components of the Language Divergence shows the interesting fact that the low value of D for the Russian/Czech pair is largely due to the similarity in phonotactics as manifested within the syllable, with isomorphy playing a much smaller role. On the other hand, the intermediate value for the Czech/German pair is accounted for — to a considerable extent — by high isomorphy of the Czech and the German phonemic systems, with phonotactics playing a decisively subordinate role in the similarity calculation. In the Russian/German result both isomorphic and isotopic differences are the largest of those calculated for any of the three pairs. In other words, our calculations generally show that Russian and Czech operate with very similar phonotactics, much more so than either Russian and German, or Czech and German. However, the qualitative similarity of the Russian and Czech phonemic inventories is less significant than the similarity of the Czech and German phonemic systems.

Since only three languages have been compared, sweeping generalizations would be unwarranted. Nevertheless, our results seem to point to at least a tentative conclusion that close genetic relationship (such as that between Russian and Czech) is likely to be manifested on the phonological level in similar phonotactics but not necessarily in very similar phonemic systems. If it can be demonstrated, in the analysis of other languages, that this conclusion is generally valid, then our method could prove useful also as a discovery procedure in establishing the probability of genetic relationship between two languages.

On the other hand, our results can also be cautiously interpreted as possibly pointing to a *Sprachbund* phenomenon. Czech and German, two languages which have been in geographic proximity and in close contact for centuries, manifest the greatest similarity in phonemic inventory of the three languages compared. In this connection, it may be also useful to recall that important developments in the formation of modern standard German took place in the eastern part of Central Germany and that the language of the Imperial Chancellery in Prague played a role in the early history of standard German.

Our calculations and tentative conclusions have been based only on three languages which represent two branches of the Indo-European family. Obviously, much more work with both Indo-European and non-Indo-European languages would be necessary to extend the conclusions and to corroborate our findings. Some work along these lines is already in progress and George K. Monroe is currently engaged in a preliminary analysis of the syllabic structure of English, using the procedures outlined here. But only when a larger number of languages has been subjected to a rigorous quantitative analysis can a more sophisticated phonological typology be elaborated and the significance of our procedures for historical and comparative linguistics more definitely evaluated.

BIBLIOGRAPHY

Avanesov, R. I., *Russkoe literaturnoe proiznošenie* (Moscow, 1954).

Avanesov, R. I., *Fonetika sovremennogo russkogo literaturnogo jazyka* (Moscow, 1956).

Avanesov, R. I., and S. I. Ožegov, *Russkoe literaturnoe proiznošenie i udarenie. Slovar´-spravočnik* (Moscow, 1960).

Axmanova, O. S., I. A. Mel´čuk, E. V. Padučeva, R. M. Frumkina, *O točnyx metodax issledovanija jazyka* (Moscow, 1961).

Bryzgunova, E. A., *Praktičeskaja fonetika i intonacija russkogo jazyka* (Moscow, 1963).

Buning, Jurgens J. E. and C. H. van Schooneveld, *The Sentence Intonation of Contemporary Standard Russian as a Linguistic Structure* (The Hague, 1961).

Cherry, E. Colin, Morris Halle, and Roman Jakobson, "Toward the Logical Description of Languages in their Phonemic Aspect", *Language*, 29 (1953) 34-46.

Cherry, E. Colin, *On Human Communication* (New York, 1961).

Chlumský, Josef, *Česká kvantita, melodie a přízvuk* (Prague, 1928).

Chomsky, Noam, *Syntactic Structures* (The Hague, 1957a).

Chomsky, Noam, Review of C. F. Hockett, A Manual of Phonology, *International Journal of American Linguistics*, 23 (1957b) 223-234.

Chomsky, Noam, Review of R. Jakobson and M. Halle, Fundamentals of Language, *International Journal of American Linguistics*, 23 (1957c) 234-242.

Chomsky, Noam, *Current Issues in Linguistic Theory* (The Hague, 1964).

Chomsky, Noam, *Aspects of the Theory of Syntax* (Cambridge, Mass., 1965).

Chomsky, Noam, "Linguistic Theory", *Northeast Conference on the Teaching of Foreign Languages* (New York, 1966) 43-49.

Chomsky, Noam and Morris Halle, "Some Controversial Questions in Phonological Theory", *Journal of Linguistics*, 1 (1965) 97-138.

Chrétien, C. Douglas, "Genetic Linguistics and the Probability Model", *Language*, 42 (1966) 518-535.

Ellegård, Alvar, "Statistical Measurement of Linguistic Relationship", *Language*, 35 (1959) 131-156.

Fant, Gunnar, *Acoustic Theory of Speech Production* (The Hague, 1960).

Grebnev, A. A., "Fonetičeskoe i morfologičeskoe oformlenie abbreviatur v russkom jazyke", *Buletin vysoké školy ruského jazyka a literatury*, 3 (1959) 5-22.

Greenberg, Joseph H., "Historical Linguistics and Unwritten Languages", *Anthropology Today*, A. L. Kroeber, ed. (Chicago, 1953) 265-286.

Greenberg, Joseph H., "The Measure of Linguistic Diversity", *Language*, 32 (1956) 109-115.

Greenberg, Joseph, *Essays in Linguistics* (Chicago, 1957).

Greenberg, Joseph H., "Synchronic and Diachronic Universals in Phonology", *Language*, 42 (1966) 508-517.

Grimes, Joseph E., "Measures of Linguistic Divergence", *Proceedings of the Ninth International Congress of Linguists* (The Hague, 1964) 44-50.

Hála, Bohuslav, *Slabika, její podstata a vývoj* (Prague, 1956).

Hála, Bohuslav, *Uvedení do fonetiky češtiny na obecně fonetickém základě* (Prague, 1962).

Hála, Bohuslav, ed., *Výslovnost spisovné češtiny, její základy a pravidla*, I (Prague, 1955).

Halle, Morris, "The Strategy of Phonemics", *Word*, 10 (1954) 197-209.

Halle, Morris, "In Defense of the Number Two", *Studies Presented to Joshua Whatmough* (The Hague, 1957) 65-72.

Halle, Morris, *The Sound Pattern of Russian* (The Hague, 1959).

Halle, Morris, "Phonology in Generative Grammar", *Word*, 18 (1962) 54–72.

Halle, Morris, "On the Bases of Phonology", *The Structure of Language*, J. A. Fodor and J. J. Katz, eds. (Englewood Cliffs, N. J., 1964) 324–333.

Halle, Morris and Kenneth N. Stevens, "Speech Recognition: A Model and a Program for Research", *The Structure of Language*, J. A. Fodor and J. J. Katz, eds. (Englewood Cliffs, N. J., 1964) 604–612.

Haugen, Einar, "The Syllable in Linguistic Description", *For Roman Jakobson* (The Hague, 1956) 213–221.

Heike, Georg, "Das phonologische System des Deutschen als binäres Distinktionssystem", *Phonetica*, 6 (1961) 162–176.

Herdan, Gustav, *Quantitative Linguistics* (Washington, 1964).

Hockett, Charles F., *A Manual of Phonology* (Baltimore, 1955).

Hoenigswald, Henry M., *Language Change and Linguistic Reconstruction* (Chicago, 1960).

Householder, F. W., "On Some Recent Claims in Phonological Theory", *Journal of Linguistics*, 1 (1965) 13–14.

Householder, F. W., "Phonological Theory: A Brief Comment", *Journal of Linguistics*, 2 (1966) 99–100.

Hultzén, Lee S., Joseph H. D. Allen, Jr., and Murray S. Miron, *Tables of Transitional Frequencies of English Phonemes* (Urbana, 1964).

Isačenko, A. V., *Fonetika spisovnej ruštiny* (Bratislava, 1947).

Jaglom, I. M., R. L. Dobrušin, A. M. Jaglom, "Teorija informacii i lingvistika", *Voprosy jazykoznanija*, 9 (1960) 100–110.

Jakobson, Roman, "Die Verteilung der stimmhaften und stimmlosen Geräuschlaute im Russischen", *Festschrift für Max Vasmer* (Berlin, 1956) 199–202.

Jakobson, Roman, "Mufaxxama — The 'Emphatic' Phonemes in Arabic", *Studies Presented to Joshua Whatmough* (The Hague, 1957) 105–115.

Jakobson, Roman, "Morfologičeskie nabljudenija nad slavjanskim skloneniem", *American Contributions to the Fourth International Congress of Slavicists* (The Hague, 1958) 127–156.

Jakobson, Roman, "Linguistics and Communication Theory", *Structure of Language and Its Mathematical Aspects* (Providence, 1961) 245–252.

Jakobson, Roman, *Selected Writings I: Phonological Studies* (The Hague, 1962).

Jakobson, Roman, C. Gunnar M. Fant, Morris Halle, *Preliminaries to Speech Analysis* (Cambridge, Mass., 1952 and later printings).

Jakobson, Roman and Morris Halle, *Fundamentals of Language* (The Hague, 1956).

Kohler, K. J., "Is the Syllable a Phonological Universal?", *Journal of Linguistics*, 2 (1966) 207–208.

Krámský, Jiří, "A Quantitative Typology of Languages", *Language and Speech*, 2 (1959) 75–85.

Kučera, Henry, *The Phonology of Czech* (The Hague, 1961).

Kučera, Henry, "Mechanical Phonemic Transcription and Phoneme Frequency Count of Czech", *International Journal of Slavic Linguistics and Poetics*, 6 (1963a) 36–50.

Kučera, Henry, "Entropy, Redundancy and Functional Load in Russian and Czech", *American Contributions to the Fifth International Congress of Slavists* (The Hague, 1963b) 191–219.

Kučera, Henry, "Statistical Determination of Isotopy", *Proceedings of the Ninth International Congress of Linguists* (The Hague, 1964) 713–721.

Kučera, Henry, "Distinctive Features, Simplicity and Descriptive Adequacy", *To Honor Roman Jakobson*, II (The Hague, 1967) 1114–1127.

Kučera, Henry, *Some Quantitative Lexical Analyses of Russian, Czech and English* (The Hague, 1968).

Kučera, Henry and W. Nelson Francis, *Computational Analysis of Present-Day American English* (Providence, 1967).

Kuryłowicz, J., "Contribution à la théorie de la syllabe", *Bulletin de la Société Polonaise de Linguistique*, 8 (1948) 80–114.

Lamb, Sydney M., "Prolegomena to a Theory of Phonology", *Language*, 42 (1966a) 536–573.

Lamb, Sydney M., *Outline of Stratificational Grammar* (Washington, 1966b).

Lehmann, Winfred P., *Historical Linguistics* (New York, 1962).

Ludvíková, Marie and Jiří Kraus, "Kvantitativní vlastnosti soustavy českých fonemů", *Slovo a slovesnost*, 27 (1966) 334–344.

Mandelbrot, Benoit, "On the Theory of Word Frequencies and on Related Markovian Models of Discourse", *Structure of Language and Its Mathematical Aspects* (Providence, 1961) 190–219.

Mázlová, Věra, "Jak se projevuje zvuková stránka češtiny v hláskových statistikách", *Naše řeč*, 30 (1946) 101–111 and 146–151.

Mázlová, Věra, "Une contribution à l'analyse de la langue tchèque au point de vue acoustique", *Lingua*, 2 (1949–50) 198–209.

Menzerath, Paul, *Die Architektonik des deutschen Wortschatzes* (Bonn-Hannover-Stuttgart, 1954).

Meyer-Eppler, W., *Grundlagen und Anwendungen der Informationstheorie* (Berlin-Göttingen-Heidelberg, 1959).

Miller, George A., *Language and Communication* (New York, 1951).

Miller, George A., "Some Effects of Intermittent Silence", *American Journal of Psychology*, 70 (1957) 311–314.

Miller, George A. and Noam Chomsky, "Finitary Models of Language Users", *Handbook of Mathematical Psychology*, R. D. Luce, R. R. Bush, and E. Galanter, eds., Vol. II (New York, 1963) 419–491.

Miller, George A. and Edwin B. Newman, "Tests of Statistical Explanation of the Rank-Frequency Relation for Words in Written English", *American Journal of Psychology*, 71 (1958) 209–218.

Monroe, George K., *Phonemic Transcription of Graphic Post-Base Affixes in English: A Computer Problem* (Ph.D. dissertation, Brown University, 1965).

Morciniec, Norbert, "Zur phonologischen Wertung der deutschen Affrikaten und Diphthonge", *Zeitschrift für Phonetik*, 11 (1958) 49–66.

Moulton, William G., "Juncture in Modern Standard German", *Language*, 23 (1947) 212–226.

Moulton, William G., "Syllable Nuclei and Final Consonant Clusters in German", *For Roman Jakobson* (The Hague, 1956) 372–381.

Moulton, William G., *The Sounds of English and German* (Chicago, 1962).

O'Connor, J. D. and J. L. M. Trim, "Vowel, Consonant, and Syllable — A Phonological Definition", *Word*, 9 (1953) 103–122.

Roberts, A. Hood, *A Statistical Linguistic Analysis of American English* (The Hague, 1965).

Saunders, R., "Asyllabic Residues in Russian", *Canadian Journal of Linguistics*, 11 (1966) 101–108.

Saunders, R., *Syllable Sequences in Russian* (Ph.D. dissertation, Brown University, in preparation).

Shannon, Claude E., "Prediction and Entropy of Printed English", *The Bell System Technical Journal*, 30 (1951) 50–64.

Shannon, Claude E. and W. Weaver, *The Mathematical Theory of Communication* (Urbana, 1949).

Shapiro, Michael, "On Non-distinctive Voicing in Russian", *Journal of Linguistics*, 2 (1966) 189–194.

Siebs Deutsche Hochsprache, edited by H. de Boor and P. Diels (Berlin, 1961).

Twaddell, W. F., "A Phonological Analysis of Intervocalic Consonant Clusters in German", *Actes du IV. congrès international de linguistes* (Copenhagen, 1936) 218–225.

Twaddell, W. F., "Standard German", *Anthropological Linguistics*, 1.3 (1959) 1–7.

Viëtor, Wilhelm, *Deutsches Aussprachewörterbuch* (Leipzig, 1921).

Vinokur, G., *Russkoe sceničeskoe proiznošenie* (Moscow, 1948).

Wilson, Robert D., "A Criticism of Distinctive Features", *Journal of Linguistics*, 2 (1966) 195–206.

Zipf, George K., *The Psycho-Biology of Language* (Boston, 1935).

Zipf, George K., *Human Behavior and the Principle of Least Effort* (Cambridge, Mass., 1949).

INDEX